**Polity Histories series**

Jeff Kingston, *Japan*
David W. Lesch, *Syria*
Dmitri Trenin, *Russia*
Kerry Brown, *China*

# France

**Emile Chabal**

polity

The right of Emile Chabal to be identified as Author of this Work has been asserted in accordance with the UK Copyright, Designs and Patents Act 1988.

First published in 2020 by Polity Press

Reprinted 2021

Polity Press
65 Bridge Street
Cambridge CB2 1UR, UK

Polity Press
101 Station Landing
Suite 300
Medford, MA 02155, USA

ISBN-13: 978-1-5095-3001-4
ISBN-13: 978-1-5095-3002-1 (pb)

A catalogue record for this book is available from the British Library.

Library of Congress Cataloging-in-Publication Data

Names: Chabal, Emile, author.
Title: France / Emile Chabal.
Description: Medford, MA : Polity Press, 2020. | Series: Polity histories | Includes bibliographical references and index. | Summary: "A wonderfully rich yet compact history of post-war France"-- Provided by publisher.
Identifiers: LCCN 2020013064 (print) | LCCN 2020013065 (ebook) | ISBN 9781509530014 (hardback) | ISBN 9781509530021 (paperback) | ISBN 9781509530045 (epub)
Subjects: LCSH: France--History--1945-
Classification: LCC DC400 .C47 2020 (print) | LCC DC400 (ebook) | DDC 944.083--dc23
LC record available at https://lccn.loc.gov/2020013064
LC ebook record available at https://lccn.loc.gov/2020013065

Typeset in 11 on 13 Berkeley by
Servis Filmsetting Ltd, Stockport, Cheshire
Printed and bound in the UK by TJ Books Limited

For further information on Polity, visit our website: politybooks.com

*Pour mon père, avec qui j'étais toujours auprès de mon arbre, et pour Adémar, l'enfant-roi.*

# Contents

Mainland France

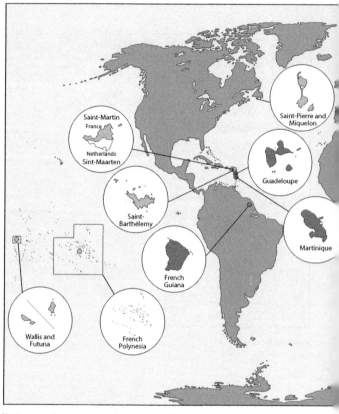

● Overseas departments and regions  ◉ Overseas communities

French Overseas Territories

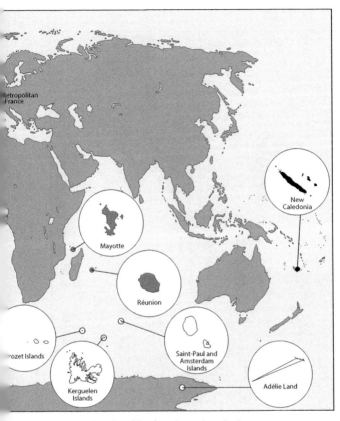

Metropolitan
France

New
Caledonia

Mayotte

Réunion

Crozet Islands

Kerguelen
Islands

Saint-Paul and
Amsterdam
Islands

Adélie Land

New Caledonia        ○ French and Southern Antarctic territories

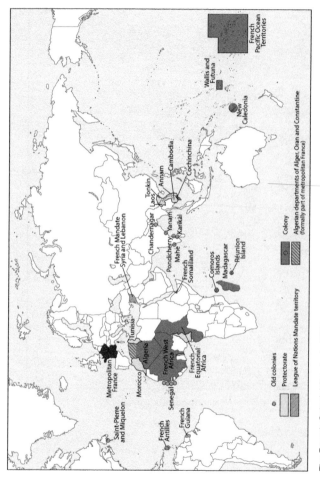

Saint-Pierre
and Miquelon

Metropolitan
France

Morocco

Tunisia

French
Antilles

Senegal

Algeria

French Mandate
Syria and Lebanon

French
Guiana

French West
Africa

French
Equatorial
Africa

Chandernagar

Pondicherry  Yanam
Mahé   Karikal

French
Somaliland

Comoros
Islands

Laos

Tonkin

Annam

Cambodia

Cochinchina

Réunion
Island

Madagascar

Wallis and
Futuna

New
Caledonia

French
Pacific Ocean
Territories

Old colonies

Protectorate

League of Nations mandate territory

Colony

Algerian departments of Alger, Oran and Constantine
(formally part of metropolitan France)

The French Colonial Empire in 1931

# Acknowledgements

Writing a short book with no endnotes has made me painfully aware of my debt to my profession and my peers. There is only one author on the title page, but this feels like a collaborative effort. Most of my arguments have been built on the scholarship of others, and I can claim very little credit for the facts and statistics I cite. For this reason, I make no apologies for the lengthy list of acknowledgements; there is no other way for me to express the depth of my gratitude to friends, colleagues and mentors for their help along the way.

I took my first steps into the field of French history thanks to Robert Tombs; his careful criticism and vast knowledge remain an inspiration to me today. I was also lucky to be supported at various points in my very early career by Sudhir Hazareesingh and Samuel Moyn. Through my research, I have met a constellation of brilliant people who have written about France and the French. These include Christian Amalvi, Arthur Asseraf, Serge Audier, Maurice Aymard, Fiona Barclay, Ed Baring, Alessandra Bitumi, Alison Carrol, Sara Casella-Colombeau, Herrick Chapman, Gwendal Châton, Sung-Eun Choi, Michael Scott Christofferson, Jackie Clarke, Martin Conway, Luis de Miranda, Mario del Pero, Nicolas Delalande, Richard Drayton, Claire Eldridge, Angéline Escafré-Dublet, Olivier Estèves, Charlotte Faucher, Mayanthi Fernando, Marion Fontaine, Stefanos Geroulanos, Robert Gildea, Jordan Girardin, Daniel Gordon, Felicity Green, Abdellali Hajjat, Ruth Harris, Nick Hewlett, Alistair Hunter, Julian Jackson, Peter Jackson, Chloe Jeffries, Jeremy Jennings, Emmanuel Jousse, Jonathan Judaken, John Keiger, Raphaëlle Khan, Nadia Kiwan, Cécile Laborde, Sonja Levsen, Itay Lotem, Kate Marsh, Hugh McDonnell, James McDougall, Emmanuel Mourlon-Druol, Ed Naylor, Alex Paulin-Booth, Timothy Peace, Thomas Pierret, Christophe Premat, Robert Priest, Christophe Prochasson, Malika Rahal, Camille Robcis, Noah Rosenblum, Yann Scioldo-Zürcher, Berny Sèbe, Jennifer Sessions, Jim Shields, Andrea Smith, Daniel Steinmetz-Jenkins, Iain Stewart, Brian Sudlow, Vincent Tiberj, Karine Varley, Natalya Vince and Laurent Warlouzet. Traces of my conversations and exchanges with these people – some fleeting, others lasting for years – can be found throughout this book. A special mention to Michael Behrent, who agreed to read the entire manuscript in record time. As always, his interventions made me think and write better.

Almost all the arguments I make in the following chapters have been tested on my students at Cambridge, Oxford and Edinburgh. In particular, the overarching structure was elaborated over many years in my Edinburgh course 'France since 1940'. Most of my students will never know that their questions, queries and frustrations were the foundation of this book. Some of them, however, deserve to be mentioned by name because their writing, research and curiosity helped me think through the big themes I have tried to address here. Thanks, then, to Rory Castle, Tom Cooper, Micaela Dempsey, Gigi Ettedgui, Lucy Gaynor, Joe Gazeley, Julia König, Charlotte Krass, Nathan Low, May Robson, Ted Sale, Patrick Soulsby and Bronagh Walsh for confirming that teachers should always listen to what their students have to say.

I owe a great deal to the various institutions that have looked after me. As a student, I was extremely fortunate to be associated with Trinity College, Cambridge, Rice University, Harvard University and the École Normale Supérieure in Paris. I was subsequently employed by Balliol College and the University of Oxford, and St John's College, Cambridge. Wherever I went, I was treated generously by peers, colleagues and administrative staff. I have been at the University of Edinburgh since 2013, and here too I have been fortunate to be a part of a community of devoted and thoughtful scholars. Of all the people I have met in Scotland, I am especially grateful to Stephan Malinowski, with whom I have had many penetrating and thought-provoking arguments about France and Europe. During my time at Edinburgh, some of my research on France has been funded by the Economic and Social Research Council under grant number ES/

N011171/1, and the Arts and Humanities Research Council under grant number AH/P008720/1.

In recent years, I have shared my ideas about contemporary France in front of inquisitive and knowledgeable audiences at the French History seminar at the Institute for Historical Research in London; the Centre for European and International Studies Research at the University of Portsmouth; the Centre for Modern and Contemporary History at the University of Birmingham; the Fondation Jean-Jaurès in Paris; the University of St Andrews; the University of Oxford; the Center for European Studies at Harvard University; the Center for International Research in the Humanities and Social Sciences at New York University; the Middle East Study Group at the University of Hull; the Museum für Kunst und Gewerbe in Hamburg; the Goethe Institut Kultursymposium in Weimar; the Franco-Scottish Society; the Centre d'Histoire de Sciences Po, Paris; the Université de Montpellier-III; the University of Aberdeen; Stockholm University; the Institut Français d'Écosse; and the Université de Lille-III. My sincerest thanks to everyone for their comments and feedback, all of which have found their way into this book somehow.

Finally, I want to express my heartfelt gratitude to my small but devoted family. Without my wife Akhila and my mother Farzana, I would not have been able to complete this – or any other – book. Only they know how important they are to my intellectual and mental health. This book is dedicated to my father, the first French person I ever met, and to little Adémar, who will soon have to grapple with some paradoxes of his own.

# Chronology

*The focus of this book is on the period from 1940 to the present, but readers may find it helpful to know about some of the key events that took place before this time. This timeline therefore starts with the French Revolution of 1789, which is usually considered the foundational moment of modern French history.*

| | |
|---|---|
| July 1789 | The French Revolution begins with the storming of the Bastille on 14 July. |
| 1791–1804 | The Haitian Revolution. |

### 1792–1804: First Republic

| | |
|---|---|
| September 1792 | Abolition of the monarchy and foundation of the First Republic. |
| 1793–1794 | The period of violence known as La Terreur (The Terror). |
| November 1799 | General Napoleon Bonaparte overthrows the French Directory in the Coup of 18 Brumaire. |
| May 1804 | Napoleon is declared emperor and announces the end of the First Republic; in its place, he inaugurates the First Empire. |
| June 1815 | Napoleon is defeated at Waterloo and the First Empire comes to an end; the monarchy is restored. |
| July 1830 | The July Revolution; King Charles X is deposed and replaced by Louis-Philippe, Duke of Orléans. |

## 1848–1851: Second Republic

| | |
|---|---|
| February 1848 | The February Revolution forces Louis-Philippe to abdicate; foundation of the Second Republic. |
| December 1851 | Louis Napoleon Bonaparte is crowned Emperor Napoleon III, thereby bringing the Second Republic to an end. |
| 1851–1870 | The Second Empire. |
| July 1870–May 1871 | Franco-Prussian War. |

## 1870–1940: Third Republic

| | |
|---|---|
| September 1870 | Foundation of the Third Republic during the Siege of Paris. |
| March–May 1871 | Paris Commune. |
| December 1905 | The legal separation of Church and State. |
| July 1914–November 1918 | First World War. |
| May 1936–April 1938 | The Popular Front government of Léon Blum, a left-wing coalition of radicals, socialists and communists. |
| June 1940 | The fall of France, which is followed by the Nazi occupation of northern France and the establishment of the Vichy administration in the southern 'free' zone. |
| November 1942 | The Nazis invade and occupy the southern 'free' zone. |
| August 1944 | Liberation of Paris. |

## 1946–1958: Fourth Republic

| | |
|---|---|
| October 1946 | The adoption of the constitution of the Fourth Republic. |
| March 1947–February 1949 | Unsuccessful anti-colonial uprising in Madagascar. |
| April 1951 | The Treaty of Paris establishes the European Coal and Steel Community. |
| May 1954 | The French army is defeated at Dien Bien |

|                  | Phu; the French formally withdraw from Indochina in August 1954. |
| November 1954    | The Algerian War begins. |
| March 1956       | Tunisia and Morocco become independent. |
| March 1957       | The Treaty of Rome establishes the European Economic Community. |
| May 1958         | Charles de Gaulle is invited to form a new government; he becomes president in January 1959. |

### 1958–present: Fifth Republic

| October 1958     | The adoption of the constitution of the Fifth Republic. |
| 1958–1960        | Independence of all the territories formerly part of French West Africa (AOF) and French Equatorial Africa (AEF). |
| February 1960    | France tests its first nuclear bomb in the Algerian Sahara. |
| March 1962       | De Gaulle signs the Évian Accords that end the Algerian War. |
| May–June 1968    | Widespread student and worker protests across France. |
| June 1969        | De Gaulle resigns as president; he is replaced by Georges Pompidou. |
| October 1973     | The first global oil crisis. |
| 1974–1981        | Presidency of the liberal Valéry Giscard d'Estaing (one term). |
| January 1975     | The 'Loi Veil' legalizes abortion. |
| 1981–1995        | Presidency of the socialist François Mitterrand (two terms). |
| March 1983       | After two years of left-wing social and economic reforms, Mitterrand announces a policy of austerity. |
| 1984             | Unemployment rate exceeds 10% for the first time since the Second World War. |

| | |
|---|---|
| September 1992 | In a referendum, the French narrowly support the adoption of the Maastricht Treaty. |
| 1995–2007 | Presidency of the centre-right Jacques Chirac (two terms). |
| December 1999 | Introduction of the euro. |
| April 2002 | Jean-Marie Le Pen, the leader of the extreme right Front National party, reaches the second round of the presidential election. |
| March 2004 | Promulgation of a law banning conspicuous religious symbols in state schools. |
| May 2005 | In a referendum, the French reject a proposed European Constitution; as a result, the entire project is abandoned. |
| October– November 2005 | Major riots in French cities in response to police violence. |
| 2007–2012 | Presidency of the centre-right Nicolas Sarkozy (one term). |
| March 2011 | France leads the NATO intervention in Libya. |
| March 2011 | After a referendum in 2009, the island of Mayotte in the Indian Ocean becomes France's 101st *département*. |
| 2012–2017 | Presidency of the socialist François Hollande (one term). |
| January 2013– July 2014 | French intervention in Mali. |
| May 2013 | Legalization of same-sex marriage (*le mariage pour tous*). |
| 2015–2016 | A series of Islamist terrorist attacks on the offices of *Charlie Hebdo* magazine in January 2015, a number of locations in Paris in November 2015, and in Nice in July 2016. |
| 2017–present | Presidency of the liberal Emmanuel Macron. |
| November 2018 | Start of the *gilets jaunes* (yellow vests) protests. |

# Introduction:
# A Paradoxical Nation

France is a country bristling with paradoxes. It harbours global ambitions, but it invests huge amounts of money in supporting minor arts festivals in small villages. It is the undisputed home of revolutionary politics, but it has been overwhelmingly governed by conservatives in the last two centuries. It is a land synonymous with strikes and labour unrest, but it has one of the lowest rates of unionization in Europe. It is one of the world's most advanced capitalist economies, but almost half of French people say they are opposed to the capitalist system. It is a place where citizens are deeply attached to their state, but do not hesitate to go into the street to protest the state's irresponsibility. And it is a country in which millions of immigrants live, but which has one of the longest-standing extreme right movements in the Western world.

To outsiders, these paradoxes can be infuriating. Every society has contradictions, but those of the French provoke an unusually intense reaction. Eventually, all but the most passionate Francophiles end up complaining about French 'hypocrisy'. The problem is usually one of dashed expectations. Starry-eyed left-wing students, taken in by the legacy of the French Revolution, the Paris Commune or the protests of 1968, come up short when they realize just how conservative the French are. Grand liberal reformers dream about the potential for France to become a truly great economy, only to despair at the apparent rigidity of the country's administrative structures. Young scholars inspired by the great French tradition of feminist writing are immediately annoyed to find that rigid gender norms and sexism are still a part of everyday life. Even casual tourists experience some form of disillusionment. The picture-postcard image of France is one of fine dining, haute couture, beautiful architecture and people who belong on the set of a glamorous French film. But many French people eat hamburgers, dress in baggy joggers and do their groceries in warehouse-like hypermarkets – and almost none of them look like Brigitte Bardot.

To some extent, the French have themselves to blame for this persistent disappointment. From the nineteenth century onwards, they relentlessly packaged their cities, landscapes, gastronomy, wine and style for foreign and domestic consumption. This was usually accompanied by lofty rhetoric about France's 'genius', 'grandeur' or 'civilizing mission', to which Europe and large parts of the world were subjected during periods of war or colonial conquest. In the realm of culture, too, the French exported their language, literary heritage and model of intellectual engagement. For much of the twentieth century, Paris was considered to be the world's pre-eminent cultural capital. Anyone who aspired to be an intellectual in Prague or Dakar was expected to know something about Émile Zola or Jean-Paul Sartre. This naturally meant that foreigners developed strong preconceptions about France. Still today, those who know the country find it hard to be neutral. They either love it, hate it or feel both emotions at the same time.

The French, of course, have rarely conformed to the elevated image people have had of them. There has been a yawning gap between the grand ideals they are supposed to embody and the messy reality. For every moment of 'greatness' in modern French history, there have been at least as many ugly ideological clashes, national humiliations and violent civil conflicts. Indeed, many of the most stirring invocations of France's universal principles and historical destiny have come during or after moments of bitter political disagreement. The high rhetoric has usually been a desperate attempt to paper over irreconcilable divisions within French society. To take only one example, France's long-standing obsession with national unity is often interpreted as a consequence of nationalist ideologies that go back to the early modern period, but it is at least as much a product of a profoundly disunited citizenry. Every person, party or movement that has tried to govern France has quickly realized that, rather than come together around common goals, the French are often at loggerheads with each other and sceptical of the grandiose oratory of those who rule them. Over time, this has led to one of the most visible paradoxes of modern French history, namely a state that repeatedly insists on an ideal of national unity and tries to impose it on a people who are often unable to agree on the most basic principles of citizenship.

For the historian, it is tempting to try to explain away these myriad contradictions and inconsistencies. Many books that provide an overview of twentieth-century French history offer a strong and coherent chronology built around wars, presidents and republics. Others proceed thematically by looking at different groups within French society or specific problems and debates. I have tried to do something a little different. Rather than treat paradox as a side-effect of France's divided past, I have used it as a lens through which to understand the way the French have thought about politics, society and culture. In this book, I explore where France's paradoxes have come from and why the country has struggled to live up to the image it has had of itself. I start from the basic assumption that most social processes and political events look different depending on who is talking about them. This is especially true of events like the Nazi occupation, the decolonization of Algeria or the protests of 1968, which gave rise to sharply conflicting memories, and incompatible historical interpretations. By acknowledging that these sorts of events were paradoxical from the very beginning, we can begin to explain why they happened – and why they proved so difficult to remember. In this way, paradox appears not as a form of hypocrisy but as a logical outcome of France's fractured and complex history.

I am hardly the first scholar of France to identify paradox as a major theme of French history. In his classic five-volume study of France from 1848 to 1945, published in the mid-1970s, the historian Theodore Zeldin used binary opposites to structure his entire text. The titles of each volume – *Ambition and Love, Intellect and Pride, Taste and Corruption, Politics and Anger, Anxiety and Hypocrisy* – were designed to capture the contradictory aspects of French life. More recently, the historian Sudhir Hazareesingh has suggested that binary opposites have been a constitutive part of French thought since the Enlightenment, a legacy of a Cartesian tendency to think in rational and abstract terms about philosophical problems. In the same vein, a rich English-language literature about contemporary French republicanism and a stimulating French-language literature about the emergence of democracy have highlighted a range of paradoxes and unresolved tensions in French history.

I build on some of these insights by bringing them into the post-war period and applying them to politics and society more broadly. I address a series of important – and unresolved – questions about contemporary France. Why do the French cling to a vision of global power despite a succession of military defeats and the collapse of their imperial ambitions? Why has the legacy of French colonialism provoked such acrimonious memory wars? Why are the French so attached to a 'republican' political ideal that seems to be morally and historically bankrupt? Why do so many French voters still long for a great leader to solve their problems, despite their open hostility to a political system that is more presidential than almost any other? Why are the French so obsessed with the state? I will not pretend that this book provides any definitive answers to these questions. But it does offer clues as to why they should be questions in the first place.

To get at some of the underlying patterns and processes that have shaped France, I have chosen to structure my six chapters around some of the most striking paradoxes of French history since 1940. The first chapter explores the French experience and memory of the Second World War. I suggest that the war gave rise to two conflicting tendencies: on the one hand, a lingering sense of defeat, which was a result of the fall of France and the subsequent Nazi occupation; on the other, a vigorous spirit of 'resistance', which took many forms during and after the war. The paradox of a country that lived both with the scars of defeat and the promise of resistance explains the diverging responses to the huge social and political transformations that took place after the war. The second chapter introduces another important context for understanding post-war France: the history of colonial conquest and the powerful anti-colonial reaction to which it gave rise. This long predated the Second World War, but the post-war period saw the conflict between colonial and anti-colonial narratives come to a head, often in moments of extreme violence. The end result of this unsustainable paradox was the almost total collapse of the French empire in the early 1960s and an angry, multi-generational struggle over colonial memory.

In chapter 3, I tackle the period now commonly known as the 'Trente Glorieuses' – the 'Thirty Glorious Years' of post-war economic growth. This sets the stage for one of the most familiar paradoxes of contemporary French politics: the contrast between the country's supposedly 'great' destiny and the hard realities of economic contraction since the 1970s. The question of whether France has (or has not) been in decline in recent decades is guaranteed to incite polemic, but the only way to understand present-day anxieties about France's place in the world is by exploring ideas of 'grandeur' that have their roots in post-war reconstruction and its most famous politician, Charles de Gaulle. The fourth chapter brings to the fore one of the best-known political cleavages in the modern world: the clash between left and right. These terms were first used during the French Revolution and they continued to resonate after the Second World War. Today, the left–right divide has lost some of its intensity, but it remains a vital part of the story of post-war France.

The final two chapters address paradoxes that have become increasingly visible in French public life in the twenty-first century. The first of these is tied to

French republicanism, a set of political values that form the basis of French political culture. In chapter 5, I discuss the glaring disparity between the most important values of French republicanism and the inequalities of French society. These disparities – and the way people have responded to them – offer a unique insight into the way the French have navigated the gap between ideals and reality. The second contemporary paradox relates to the tension between France's strong local traditions and its unashamedly global outlook. As I show in chapter 6, few paradoxes are as acute today as the one between a French citizenry that wants more local democracy and a state that wants to be a European and global power. As the recent *gilets jaunes* protests clearly demonstrate, this paradox has not been resolved, and may well become more acute in future.

It will be obvious that these six chapters cannot do justice to the richness of French history since 1940. This is a very short book, and I have had to omit an enormous number of themes, personalities and events. I particularly regret that I could not say more about intellectual and cultural debates, environmental history, rural life, cinema and music, and the family. I have made a conscious decision to focus on politics, mostly because politics touches almost every aspect of life in France, but even here I do not pretend to have covered each topic in detail. Instead, I offer a series of arguments about how France works and how the French think. While many of these run through the whole book, the chapters do not necessarily have to be read as a single, chronological narrative that begins with France's defeat in 1940 and ends with the *gilets jaunes* protests in 2018 and 2019. It is also possible to treat each chapter as an essay on a specific problem within contemporary French history, especially because several of them begin with a discussion of people, events and histories that predate 1940. There is a basic timeline at the start of the book to help readers navigate the chronology of modern France.

I should stress that the point of this book is not to offer a definitive account of contemporary French history. My aim is more modest. I want to use some of the exciting new work that is being published in the field to shine an unfamiliar light on familiar stories. I am assuming that my readers will have some interest in France, either as students, tourists, residents or aficionados of French culture. If this is the case, then I hope my arguments will stimulate further reading and reflection. I will be equally happy if they lead to disagreement and debate. Writing about contemporary France is a sure way to court controversy, and I expect that my ideas will be challenged by my readers and my colleagues. Nevertheless, if the only result of my book is to make the French seem a little less paradoxical, I will consider it a job well done.

# 1

# Defeat and Resistance

It is impossible to overstate the impact of the fall of
France in June 1940. When the Germans invaded, it
was the third time in less than a century that France
had been occupied by its neighbour. In 1870–1, the
Franco-Prussian War ended with a humiliating defeat
for the French armies, the collapse of Napoleon
III's Second Empire, the annexation of the eastern
territories of Alsace and Lorraine, and a violent urban
insurrection in the form of the Paris Commune. After
nursing their broken pride for almost half a century,
the French were given the chance to redeem themselves in 1914. But the First World War was a poisoned
chalice. The Allied armies did eventually prevail – and
many of the territories lost in 1870 were returned to
France – but the war took an immense toll on French
society. More than 7.8 million French soldiers were
called up and 1.5 million of them died on the killing
fields of Verdun, the Marne and the Somme. Never
had so many French people perished in a single conflict. The human costs were profound, and, still today,
almost every French town and village has a memorial
to those who died.

It is hardly a surprise, then, that the terrifying spec-
tacle of the rapidly advancing Nazi army in late spring

1940 struck fear into the French population. Hundreds of thousands of people in northern France ran from their homes. Horses, carts, cars and vans clogged the roads as families fled an enemy they knew and feared. The French army, which had been preparing for just this eventuality, was completely outmanoeuvred; its tactics failed, and its soldiers were unable to halt the inexorable progress of the Wehrmacht. With the chastening British retreat at Dunkirk – a retreat that was only possible thanks to the sacrifice of French soldiers – the French army was left to its fate. It withdrew, until it could withdraw no more. Paris fell on 14 June, and, on 22 June, Philippe Pétain signed the armistice agreement that divided France into a northern occupied zone and a southern 'free' zone. In a mere six weeks, one of continental Europe's great powers had been humbled, its sophisticated armies scattered and its government dismantled.

### In the Shadow of Defeat

One of the paradoxes of the fall of France was that it was both an enormous surprise and an event foretold. Clearly, no one expected the tactics of the French army to fail so spectacularly. Few could have foreseen the speed with which the Nazis crushed their opponents. Although the subjugation of Czechoslovakia in 1938 and the obliteration of Poland in 1939 had given ample warning of the potential of Hitler's army, it was the fall of France that symbolized German military dominance over Europe. Henceforth, no European power would underestimate the ruthless efficiency of the German military machine.

But, if the shock of 1940 was real, the fear of defeat was nothing new. For decades, many French people believed their country had been going awry. Most conservatives, for instance, abhorred the parliamentary regime of the Third Republic, which had been in place since 1870, and were neither surprised nor particularly upset to see it fall apart in 1940. Those of a more fascist or anti-Semitic bent were equally nonplussed at the collapse of the Third Republic. They were not going to mourn the passing of a political system that had made it possible for a socialist and communist Popular Front government to take power in 1936, under the stewardship of the country's most famous Jew, Léon Blum. On the opposite side of the political spectrum, French communists had maintained since the 1920s that France was a bourgeois, capitalist society. For them, the economic depression of the 1930s and the rise of fascism in Europe were harbingers of the terminal crisis of capitalism, and the defeat of 1940 was a logical outcome of this process. Even those of a moderate, liberal bent – many of whom had been the most enthusiastic supporters of the Third Republic – had spent years bemoaning the rigidity of France's institutions and the inability of the French to adapt, not least to the reality of German economic development.

The fall of France laid bare these divisions. As

many had predicted, the parliamentary institutions of the Third Republic were unable to survive the defeat. In an act of collective suicide, the members of the Assemblée nationale voted 569 to 80 (with 20 abstentions) to hand 'full control' of government to Pétain on 10 July 1940. This piece of legislation brought a *de facto* end to the Third Republic. In so doing, it confirmed what many on the right and left of the political spectrum had long suspected, namely that parliamentary democracy had run its course. It also fitted a much longer pattern in modern French history of authoritarian regimes dissolving parliamentary structures. In 1799, Napoleon Bonaparte terminated the French Revolution in a dramatic coup d'état. Just over 50 years later, his nephew Charles-Louis Napoléon Bonaparte repeated the trick by bringing the democratic revolutionary wave of 1848 to a close with a coup d'état in 1851. Even if the circumstances in 1940 were not as favourable as those of 1799 or 1851, the same pattern played out again, as Pétain took the helm of what was left of the French government. Most French people hoped that he would be a reassuring leader who would raise the country from the depths of defeat and occupation.

Unfortunately, this is not what happened. For a start, the independence of the French government – now based in Vichy, in the southern 'free' zone – was severely compromised. Nominally, the Vichy regime administered metropolitan French territory and the entire French colonial empire; it also maintained its own civil service, army and police. In practice, Paris and the most economically productive regions of northern and eastern France were under direct German control, while the Vichy regime gradually lost its grip on far-flung colonial territories under pressure from the Free French resistance, the British and the Japanese. To make matters worse, the British had paralysed the French fleet in order to stop it falling into German hands, most famously in the devastating attack on the naval base at Mers-el-Kébir in July 1940, and the French army had been effectively neutralized by the direct German occupation of the entire Atlantic coastline. This amputation of France's military might was followed by the systematic exploitation of the French economy for the Nazi war effort. Factories and equipment were repurposed to produce arms and supplies, and French workers were used to fill the insatiable German demand for highly skilled labour, especially after the implementation of the Service du travail obligatoire (STO, Obligatory Labour Service) in February 1943. If the occupation of France was relatively benign, at least in comparison to the brutality of Nazi rule in Eastern Europe, there was no mistaking the Nazis' main purpose. They intended to bleed the country dry.

The growing privations of daily life – the rations, the shortages, the requisitioning of food and men – did not stop the ideologues of the Vichy regime from announcing their intention to begin a 'National Revolution' to redress France. The aim was to combine

elements of Catholic traditionalism, secular conserv-
atism and homegrown fascism in order to create an
integrated, harmonious society that would be struc-
tured around the cardinal values of 'travail, famille,
patrie' (work, family, nation). The architects of the
Vichy state intended to use the unusual circumstances
of defeat and subjugation to recreate France. And, by
transforming the famous republican slogan of 'liberté,
égalité, fraternité' (liberty, equality, fraternity), they
explicitly sought to position themselves within a long
tradition of counter-revolution.

For a while, it seemed to be working. The Vichy
regime benefited from a certain degree of popu-
larity, and most French people accepted the realities of German occupation. It helped that almost
all opponents of collaboration – whether communist or right-wing nationalist – were either shot,
detained, deported, in exile or forced into silence.
Nevertheless, collaboration took place at every level
of French society, from civil servants and university
professors to small business owners and prostitutes.
There was little outright resistance to German occupation in the north, even less to the authoritarian
policies of the Vichy regime in the south. The authorities in both zones benefited from a widespread culture of distrust, as many people turned a blind eye
to the persecution of Jews and other 'undesirables',
and some even denounced the supposed misdeeds
of their friends, neighbours and family members.
Tacit and explicit forms of social control, as well as

a good deal of war fatigue, gave the appearance of social consensus.

Unlike in 1799 or 1851, however, there was no getting away from the fact that this anti-democratic revolution was built on top of defeat. While Pétain could argue in 1940 that the Vichy regime was the best option in a bad situation, these claims became increasingly tenuous as the war dragged on. The imposition of direct German rule over the whole of metropolitan France in November 1942 and, especially, the implementation of the STO highlighted the degree to which the Vichy regime was powerless to prevent the exploitation of the country, its resources and its people. Farmers began to hoard their food; young labour conscripts started to abscond; and disgruntled workers turned towards the small groups of violent resisters scattered across provincial France. With the progress of the Allied war effort, it seemed as if the tide might be turning. Shunned by its supporters and detested by its opponents, the Vichy regime felt its legitimacy ebb away.

By 1944, it was clear that the Nazis' days were numbered. Just as the fall of France had announced the beginning of the 'real' war in the West, so the two decisive engagements of the Western Front in 1944 – the Allied landings in Normandy in June and the Côte d'Azur in August – marked the beginning of the end of the conflict. On the face of it, both engagements appeared to be an unqualified success for the French since they led to the liberation of the country and the final defeat of Hitler. Helped by small, coordinated resistance activities, the Allied armies slowly pushed back the same army that had triumphantly driven into northern France more than four years earlier. In a moment of immense significance, the newly proclaimed leader of France – Charles de Gaulle – gave a rousing speech from the Hôtel de Ville in Paris on 25 August to celebrate the liberation of the capital city. His was a call to arms and an exhortation. He urged his fellow citizens to show themselves 'worthy of France' and its great history. It was exactly what the French needed to hear after the humiliation of occupation.

Yet the unravelling of the German occupation could not hide the harsh legacies of defeat. The scars of 1940 were unmistakable. At the end of the war, France's towns and cities, above all in the north, had been flattened by bombing. The country had lost 20% of its housing stock, with countless other residential buildings, factories, warehouses and workshops damaged in battle. Agricultural production had collapsed. Most communication networks – from telephones to railways – were in terrible condition. There were human consequences, too. Mob violence broke out across France after the Liberation, as self-appointed vigilante groups took revenge on alleged collaborators. In total, almost 9,000 were killed in extra-judicial violence. Elsewhere, women accused of *collaboration horizontale* (horizontal collaboration, or having sex with the enemy) were paraded through the streets with shaved heads and civil servants who had served the Vichy regime hurriedly burnished their resistance credentials in the hope that they would be rehabilitated and allowed to continue working for the state. Even at a geopolitical level, France had lost its place at the high table of global diplomacy. De Gaulle never forgave the British and Americans for not inviting him to participate in the Yalta and Potsdam conferences in 1945 that set the future shape of Europe.

The French made numerous attempts to shake off these lingering embarrassments of defeat in the years after 1944. The Gouvernement provisoire de la République Française (GPRF, Provisional Government of the French Republic), which ran France from June 1944 to October 1946, annulled the Vichy regime and announced an ambitious programme for the reconstruction of the country. The variety of different political tendencies represented in the provisional government – including communists – meant that the proposals had a more radical and social tinge than any other legislative package since the Popular Front of 1936. The promulgation of a new constitution in October 1946 saw the birth of the Fourth Republic, which was supposed to establish a robust parliamentary democracy, untainted by the shameful capitulation of its predecessor.

A symbol of this new dawn was the enfranchisement of women. France was one of the last European countries to give women the vote, and their belated inclusion in the political community in 1945 marked a definitive break with the past. Alongside an expanded franchise, the politicians and administrators of the Fourth Republic set about implementing some of the reforms promised by the GPRF. Many businesses were (re)nationalized, the tax system was modernized and a vast new social security system was established, part of which involved building hundreds of thousands of new social housing units from the mid-1950s onwards. As many historians of the period now recognize, the reconstruction of France in the decades after the Second World War was an immense peaceful revolution that transformed the character, structure, social relations and culture of France. This collective effort did much to erase the ugly memories of the so-called *années noires* (dark years) of the German occupation.

But memories of the war persisted just below the surface. Except for a few prominent trials of political and intellectual figures, of which the most famous was that of the writer Robert Brasillach, who was executed in February 1945, most people suspected of collaboration were quietly rehabilitated thanks to one of the three amnesty laws of 1947, 1951 and 1953. The administrative architecture and personnel of the Fourth Republic were virtually unchanged from those of the Vichy regime, both at a national level and at a local level. Meanwhile, many victims, especially those who had been prisoners of war or forced labourers, demanded recognition by the state, as did prominent (usually male) members of the various resistance movements. Their attempts to fix a positive memory of unified French resistance to the occupation obscured the troubling reality of a population that had often worked with the Nazis, even when it meant acquiescing in the persecution of the Jews. For their part, French Jews who survived the Holocaust avoided public commemoration, preferring private religious ceremonies to remember the tragedy that had befallen their community.

Underneath the veneer of reconstruction, then, many French people continued to carry the weight of 1940. For the most part, this was invisible, but occasionally it exploded in spectacular fashion. As we will see later, it was the obsessive desire on the part of the French military high command to avoid a repeat of 1940 that led to the catastrophic and protracted military engagements in Indochina and in Algeria in the 1950s and 1960s. The infamous French defeat at the battle of Dien Bien Phu in spring 1954 was a distillation of these memories; this was the first time that a major European imperial power had been beaten in open combat by a supposedly ill-trained indigenous guerrilla force. It was a similar story in Algeria, where the French tried to avoid a repeat, not only of 1940, but also of 1954. In the end, they only succeeded in enflaming the multiple layers of anti-colonial violence that led to one of the bloodiest wars of decolonization anywhere in the world. De Gaulle tried his best to portray the Évian Accords, which brought an end to the Algerian War in March 1962, as a victory for

French diplomacy. The reality was that this was yet another defeat. Try as they might, the French were not able to shake off the legacy of 1940.

It was perhaps inevitable that, after engulfing the colonies, the spectre of defeat would eventually return to haunt metropolitan France. Already, the mixed memories of the war ran as a thread through the protests of 1968. The baby-boom generation at the forefront of the demonstrations began to demand that their parents explain the silences surrounding collaboration and the deportation of the Jews. The more radical amongst them compared de Gaulle to Hitler, and chanted 'we are all German Jews', while riot police tried to keep the unruly mob at bay. But state repression and censorship were not enough to contain the contradictions of defeat. In the 1970s and 1980s, the French were forced to confront the uncomfortable realities of occupied France through a series of epoch-making films and documentaries. The most famous of these was Marcel Ophuls's four-hour epic *Le chagrin et la pitié* (*The Sorrow and the Pity*, 1969), which coolly chronicled stories of collaboration during the war, from the music halls of Paris to the living rooms of the provincial bourgeoisie. The film was deemed so incendiary that it was banned from French TV on its release, but this only contributed to its underground success. It ended up being screened for 87 weeks in Parisian cinemas.

In subsequent decades, the French found themselves locked into a phenomenon that the historian

Henry Rousso famously termed 'the Vichy syndrome'. What had previously appeared to be a lack of interest in the uglier aspects of France's experience during the Second World War became a veritable obsession with the exact nature of – and appropriate punishment for – collaboration. The trials of the former SS officer Klaus Barbie in 1987, and the former Vichy-era civil servants Paul Touvier in 1994 and Maurice Papon in 1998, led to lengthy judicial and public discussion over the extent of individual responsibility for the various crimes committed under Vichy. This discussion frequently exceeded the limited time period of the Second World War. Papon, for instance, stood accused of facilitating the deportation of Jews from Bordeaux during the war, but he later served as police chief in Paris at the height of the Algerian War. His stint in Paris was marked by regular police violence against Algerians that culminated in the massacre of 17 October 1961, when a march in favour of Algerian independence was brutally suppressed. The longevity of Papon's service raised difficult questions: technically, he was only on trial for his actions during the Second World War, but activists wanted to indict him for his behaviour throughout his career. In response, Papon claimed he was simply doing his job as a civil servant of the French state. His trial – and the debate it ignited – blurred the lines between Vichy and Algeria, the two most painful French defeats of the twentieth century.

Several generations have passed since the end of

the Second World War, and even the generation of the Algerian War is now largely gone. Most French citizens today have not experienced first-hand the humiliation of outright military defeat. But the fall of France in 1940 has nevertheless cast a very long shadow. It is occasionally visible in spectacular public controversies, such as when Emmanuel Macron defended Pétain after a military commemoration ceremony in November 2018. More than specific events, however, the shadow of 1940 has defined the contours of contemporary French political life. As we will see throughout this book, it underpins the repeated desire on the part of the French to participate in the very highest levels of global diplomacy, despite the country's obviously second-tier status. And it explains the sense of anxious, wounded pride that pervades the writings of those commentators who lament the 'decline' of France. There may not be many military battles left to fight, but the French continue to remain sensitive to anything that might, in the words of the philosopher Alain Finkielkraut, look like 'la défaite de la pensée [the defeat of thought]'.

## *The Spirit of Resistance*

The idea of resistance in France was not born during the Second World War. It had a much longer genealogy. In 1793, at the height of the French Revolution, the French people were summoned to resist the onslaught of Europe's reactionary powers in the military *levée en masse* (mass conscription). Throughout the nineteenth century, different groups in French society tried to resist the prevailing political winds. Republicans and socialists resisted the dictatorial fantasies of Napoleon III; monarchists and Catholics resisted the godless secularism of the Third Republic; communists resisted the slow creep of the bourgeois state; and extreme right ideologues resisted the inexorable sense of French decadence after the Franco-Prussian war. After 1944, however, the term 'resistance' became overwhelmingly associated with French responses to the German occupation during the Second World War. It was during these years that the French began to refer specifically to *the* Resistance, with a capital 'R'.

This emphasis on the singularity of French wartime resistance might come as a surprise. In comparison to their Yugoslav or Polish counterparts, the actions of the French Resistance were modest. They experienced few tactical successes or tragic disasters around which to build a story of collective suffering. Moreover, as many historians have shown, the resistance to German occupation in France was, for many years, scattered and disunited. After the fall of France in 1940, the key distinction was between Free France, a network of resistance activities directed from London by de Gaulle, and the *Résistance intérieure*, the umbrella term used to describe the less coordinated resistance movements that operated inside French territory. These groups did not always share the same aims and occasionally came into direct conflict with one another. It was only in 1943 that they coalesced into a singular entity under the tutelage of de Gaulle.

This belated process of unification meant that, by the time of the Liberation, de Gaulle could argue that he was the head of *the* Resistance. Few contested his claim. Even the Americans, who had always been sceptical of his credentials, were forced to admit that he had become the country's *de facto* leader. But de Gaulle himself was aware of his own fragility. He knew that he could not take his authority for granted. His fate was tied up with that of the Resistance he purported to lead. This explains why he worked so hard to fashion the image of the Resistance to serve his political purposes. In his famous speech at the Hôtel de Ville, he told the crowd that Paris had been 'liberated by itself, liberated by its people with the help of the French army, and the support of all of France – that is to say, fighting France, the only France, the real France, eternal France'. These stirring words were mostly hyperbole. Paris had been liberated by the Allied forces, assisted by the French Resistance. While the overwhelming majority of French people were glad to see the back of the Germans, there was no such thing as a 'fighting France'. On the contrary, historians estimate that no more than 2–3% of the French population were involved in resistance activities, and there was little ideological coherence between the different groups. Once the war was over, Gaullist resisters found it very difficult to make common cause with their Communist counterparts in the GPRF. Within a year or two, the much-vaunted unity of the Resistance had collapsed.

The French Resistance was thus a myth from its very inception. After 1944, it served as both a foil for the compromises of occupation and a rousing narrative from which post-war France could draw strength. By summoning the spirit of the Resistance, de Gaulle and his successors were drawing on one of the oldest tropes of French politics: the call for unity in the face of disunity. With reports of mob violence flooding in from prefects and police in provincial France, and complex anti-colonial movements taking shape in Indochina and Algeria, the story of the Resistance was a useful vehicle for national unity. It helped cover up the ambiguities of occupation; it emphasized the agency of the French after years of subjugation; and it injected a sense of moral purpose into a period that had been dominated by amoral, pragmatic compromise. It also offered a form of rehabilitation for those who needed to atone for their actions during the war: belated 'conversions' to the Resistance offered a path to respectability. Like all post-war European societies, the French needed a story of unity and triumph in adversity as the precondition for the material and psychological reconstruction of the late 1940s and 1950s.

The myth of the Resistance reached its apogee in the 1960s. In December 1964, the ashes of Jean Moulin – a well-known resistance leader killed in 1943 – were transferred to the Panthéon, the pre-eminent burial site for France's leading public personalities. The event provided the occasion for the then culture minister, the writer André Malraux, to give one of the most moving public funeral orations of the post-war years. In a little over 20 minutes, he paid homage not only to Moulin's actions during the war, but also to the 'people of the night' and the 'people of the shadows' who formed the 'organic' resistance. In a flurry of vivid metaphors, Malraux brought to life the myth of a country united in its opposition to German rule, from the Champs Elysées to the smallest village in the Auvergne. He ended his oration by appealing to the 'youth' to imagine how they might have approached the great Moulin and, by implication, how they might have responded to the moral choices of the war. Still today, the speech stands as a masterful and beautiful exercise in collective memory.

Unfortunately, the 'youth' of the 1960s did not necessarily share Malraux's inspirational view of the Resistance. For a start, many young people had started to ask difficult questions about the behaviour of their parents during the war; they no longer believed every grand tale of resistance heroism. In addition, they had good reasons to believe that France in the 1950s and 1960s had not embodied the noble spirit of the Resistance. At home, the revolutionary promise of the GPRF's social programme had been watered down by the technocrats of the Fourth Republic and the Gaullist presidentialism of the Fifth Republic, inaugurated in 1958. Overseas, the story was worse. For a generation of anti-colonial protesters in the 1950s, the behaviour of the French army in Indochina and North Africa was nothing less than a complete reversal of roles. Where once the French army had led the resistance to Nazi rule, its exploits in the colonies now suggested the opposite. In Oran and Saigon, the French were the occupiers, brutally suppressing the legitimate resistance of colonized peoples.

As we will see again and again, this battle over the meaning of a specific concept – in this case, resistance – is one of the most striking characteristics of modern French politics. In the post-war period, the dominant meaning of resistance was that of the (wartime) Resistance. This idea of a cohesive opposition to German occupation carried within it the morality of anti-fascism, ideas about the unity of the French nation and a strong sense of the indomitable spirit of the French people. But these connotations could easily be challenged. Communists felt that they represented a more authentic anti-fascism than any Gaullist resister. Filmmakers like Ophuls, by exposing the realities of wartime collaboration, blew apart the idea that the French were unified during the occupation. And highly educated activists from the French colonies, many of whom had fought in the French army during the Second World War, could legitimately claim that the liberation of 'indomitable' France would have been impossible without the forgotten sacrifice of the colonized. The more the French state tried to fix the idea of resistance within the narrative of the Second

World War, the more people began to cast doubt on its meaning.

The most persistent attempts to reclaim the idea of resistance from its wartime mantle came from the left of the political spectrum. The left could lean on a long alternative history of resistance to the forces of reaction, from the French Revolution to the Paris Commune, and it did not hesitate to mobilize these memories in its post-war struggles. Resistance became a catch-all term for almost any protest against the state, capitalism, big business, consumer culture or political figures of the right. In 1968, the word 'Résistance!' appeared on student posters, while young *gauchiste* agitprop artists twisted the Gaullist symbol of resistance – the Cross of Lorraine – into a symbol of creeping state fascism. Elsewhere, the Parti communiste français (PCF, French Communist Party) routinely used the word 'resistance' to describe the class struggle ('la résistance prolétarienne'), and feminists in the 1970s called on women to resist patriarchy. More generally, resistance was one of the most common exhortations during left-wing marches and demonstrations, often used as a verb ('résistez!', 'résistons!'). In many cases, the object of resistance was not specified; it was enough simply to resist.

Over time, this left-wing invocation of resistance began to subvert the dominant meaning of the term. Where de Gaulle and his followers used resistance as a way of uniting the French around a common story of heroism and endurance, left-wing activists emphasized its radical and insurrectionary potential. Instead of unity, they urged their supporters to light the touchpaper of social and political revolution by resisting the diktats of the French state. They fused the imagery and symbolism of revolution – such as barricades and marches – with the moral purpose of the wartime Resistance. This combination has now become a staple of left-wing political discourse. Still today, left-wing parties and movements try to mix the languages of revolution and resistance in order to energize their supporters and recruit members. In 2014, 70 years after the liberation of France, the PCF circulated a campaign poster emblazoned with the words: 'C'est le moment de s'engager: rejoignez la résistance!' ('It's time to get involved: join the resistance!'). Unlike in 1944, when the party could claim to be the biggest party in France, by 2014 it was a minor player in French politics. But, even in such straitened circumstances, its campaign managers did not hesitate to invoke the ghosts of revolution and resistance. For the party faithful, it was as important to carry the flame of resistance as it was to win elections.

One of the consequences of these changing meanings of resistance has been the emergence of France as a global beacon of opposition to some of the most powerful political and economic tendencies of the post-war period. In the 1950s and 1960s, this was particularly visible in French relations with the United States. Although France accepted American Marshall aid to help fund reconstruction and never threatened to switch sides during the Cold War, French politicians maintained a strong anti-American stance. On the left, the PCF railed against the power of the world's pre-eminent imperialist and capitalist nation, frequently arguing in favour of hostile policies towards manifestations of American economic and political power. On the right, there were some who embraced the dynamism of post-war American capitalism, but most retained a strong sense of cultural snobbery towards the United States. De Gaulle himself shared many of these attitudes. His highly symbolic withdrawal from NATO High Command in 1966 indicated the lengths to which he was willing to go in his attempts to resist American hegemony.

In recent years, there have been numerous opportunities to replay this Franco-American rivalry. In 1993, the French were instrumental in securing the exclusion of 'cultural products' from the Uruguay Round of GATT trade talks; they argued that culture could not be subject to the same free-market rules as goods and services. In 2003, the Gaullist president Jacques Chirac and his foreign minister Dominique de Villepin vocally spearheaded the resistance to the US-led invasion of Iraq on the grounds that it would be illegitimate and unwarranted. And, since 2017, US President Donald Trump and Emmanuel Macron have regularly faced off in a series of diplomatic spats. Sceptics claim that these skirmishes have been of little consequence for the direction of France's foreign and domestic policy. This may well be true. Nevertheless, they have contributed to a sense amongst the French themselves and on the part of outsiders that France is Europe's bastion of resistance to American power.

The persistence of anti-Americanism in twenty-first-century France is tied to another important catalyst for resistance: the state of the global economy. In 2009, the Globescan polling organization released the results of a 27-country survey, which made for startling reading. By their calculations, France was the country in which the largest proportion of people believed in the need for an alternative economic system. A full 43% of French respondents agreed with the statement that free-market capitalism 'is wrong and we need another system', compared to 29% of Italians and Spaniards, 19% of Britons, 13% of Americans and only 9% of Germans. Such deep-rooted popular scepticism about capitalism, which has been reinforced by a proliferation of anti-globalization movements in France since the mid-1990s, shows how the idea of resistance has transcended its narrow wartime connotations to become one of the defining features of contemporary French politics. For many young French people today, the most important form of resistance is the global resistance to capitalism, from Paris to Santiago de Chile.

Closer to home, a posture of stubborn resistance has also come to characterize the relationship between the French people and the state that governs them. As we will see in the final chapter, the history of state–citizen relations in France is complex and dynamic, but it is enough to note here that the most common expressions of the spirit of the resistance in France today are the banners, slogans and pamphlets urging the French to resist the imposition of new taxes, regulations or reforms by the state. The *gilets jaunes* (yellow vests) movement that began in late 2018 provides a case in point. For months on end, crowds of protesters gathered every Saturday to express their dissatisfaction at the current state of France. The amorphous composition and ideological flexibility of the *gilets jaunes* made them extremely difficult to pin down, but there were a few common themes. One of these was resistance. Right from the start, the *gilets jaunes* encouraged their fellow citizens to resist a heartless state, an authoritarian president, the dominance of Paris, neo-liberalism, unfair taxation and the closure of rural surgeries. Protestors scrawled 'résistance!' onto the back of their yellow vests and spoke of the need to fight back against damaging economic reforms. In one instance, a group of protesters took the history of the Resistance literally by setting up a small marquee on the Place de la République in Paris that claimed to house the 'Conseil national de la Résistance des Gilets Jaunes'. In any other context, a reference to the wartime Conseil national de la Résistance would have seemed wholly anachronistic. But it made perfect sense to the people who did it. As far as they were concerned, they were the true heirs of Jean Moulin.

Resistance, then, has always been the necessary counterpart to defeat in post-war France. As de Gaulle well understood, the humiliations of the latter could only be rectified by the intensity of the former. But neither de Gaulle nor his successors could permanently fix the language of resistance. Time and again, they lost control of the story they were trying to tell. Anti-colonial rebels in the late 1950s, left-wing students in 1968, feminists in the 1970s and anti-globalization protesters in the 1990s each reinterpreted resistance to encompass a diversity of domestic and international struggles. In many cases, this meant jettisoning a Gaullist narrative of national unity in favour of a more urgent call to resist the inequalities of the present. On occasion, it meant directly attacking the myth of French wartime resistance as an oppressive tool of the state. Regardless of the form, every invocation of resistance in post-war France has urged the French people not to accept defeat in the face of adverse political, economic or ideological circumstances. It is this belief in the transience of defeat that connects the young resisters who blew up bridges in occupied France and the *gilets jaunes* waving anti-Macron banners. Both groups clung passionately to a spirit of resistance because they knew the alternative was the gnawing pessimism of defeat.

# 2

# Colonialism and Anti-Colonialism

At its height in around 1920, the French colonial empire covered 11.5 million square kilometres across five continents. It encompassed the mangrove swamps of French Guiana in South America, large parts of the Sahara Desert, the sticky tropical forests of Indochina in Southeast Asia and the idyllic beaches of French Polynesia in the South Pacific. Even more remarkable than this geographical diversity was the sheer variety of people who lived under French rule. Many of them never met more than a handful of French-speakers in their lives, but they were nevertheless part of a vast imperial world. Whether they knew it or not, they were connected both to each other and to a distant place called France. The process that led to the creation of such an extraordinary transnational community is one of the most important – and unsettling – aspects of modern French history. It affected the spatial, political and human meaning of France, and had profound consequences for the lives of the millions of people who were swept up in the expansion and contraction of the French empire.

## *The Rise and Fall of the French Colonial Empire*

The history of the French empire goes back many centuries. The French were one of the pre-eminent European imperial powers of the eighteenth century, but they lost most of their territories in Asia, Africa and the Americas over the course of the various wars that preceded and followed the French Revolution in 1789. As a result, historians tend to associate the modern history of the French empire with the end of the Napoleonic Wars in 1815. At this point, the French could only lay claim to a handful of overseas possessions in India, the French Antilles and various settlements along the coast of Senegal (including Dakar and Saint-Louis). These so-called 'old' colonies would subsequently have a special status within the French empire, which meant they were subject to different political and legal systems and remained more closely tied to metropolitan France.

The enormous expansion of the French empire over the course of the nineteenth century took place in stages, starting with the colonization of Algeria in 1830. This was followed by the acquisition of various Indian Ocean and Pacific Ocean islands in the 1830s and 1840s and the conquest of parts of Southeast Asia and West Africa in the 1850s and 1860s. The imperial frenzy reached its height during the Third Republic, when the French consolidated their hold over large parts of North and West Africa and what would become, in 1887, Indochina. The French further expanded their sphere of influence in the interwar years when the League of Nations placed parts of central Africa, Syria and Lebanon under French mandate. During this entire period, there were occasional voices of opposition, but the vast majority of the French elite championed the cause of imperial expansion. When it came to empire, even the bitterest political foes agreed that imperial rule was beneficial for colonizer and colonized alike.

For all the apparent consensus about its value, though, it is important to remember that there were significant differences in the military, social and political conditions across the French empire. In some cases, conquest was violent and destabilizing, as in the case of Algeria; in other cases, it was limited and superficial, as in parts of central Africa. Patterns of economic development were highly uneven. The Algerian coast, for instance, was rapidly urbanized and developed a complex, stratified society composed of European settlers, Arab Muslims and Jews. By contrast, the Algerian interior remained poor and dominated by local conflicts, often heightened by the brutal French expropriation of land. The penetration of French culture and political values was also inconsistent. In 'old' colonies like Senegal or Martinique, and in settler colonies like Algeria and New Caledonia, the French school system acted as a vehicle for the inculcation of the French language and culture. But in more isolated parts of the Sahara and central Africa, the French presence was limited to occasional visits by tax collectors, administrators and missionaries.

These inconsistencies were reflected in the variety of governing structures that existed across the French empire. By the interwar period, there were essentially three forms of colonial administration. The first was direct rule, where overseas territories were managed directly by the French government. The best example of this was the three coastal *départements* of Algeria, which were – in theory – an extension of metropolitan France, no different from Corsica or Brittany. The 'old' colonies, too, had a similar relationship to the metropole, albeit without the benefits of being formally attached to France like Algeria. The second form of government was indirect rule, with substantial power devolved to local colonial authorities. This was the system in place in territories such as Madagascar, Indochina, Afrique Occidentale Française (AOF, French West Africa) and Afrique Équatoriale Française (AEF, French Equatorial Africa). Lastly, there were territories that had a degree of autonomy, while still under a French sphere of influence. These included the protectorates of Morocco and Tunisia, and the parts of the Middle East under French mandate control.

The chaos of the Second World War, which did so much to destabilize the politics of metropolitan France, was a watershed moment for the empire. The problems began immediately with the fall of France in 1940. Although Pétain signed an armistice agreement on behalf of France, it was not clear whether this also applied to the French empire. Colonial administrators in Algiers, Hanoi and Pondicherry were left in the difficult position of having to declare their allegiance either to Pétain's state or to some other, as-yet non-existent form of government-in-exile. Initially, this decision was made almost by default. In the absence of any alternative government, the whole of the French empire came under the control of Vichy France, a move that was facilitated by the long-standing right-wing and anti-republican tendencies amongst France's colonial and settler elites. Nevertheless, the French empire quickly became a potent political and military battleground. As the months wore on, both Vichy and de Gaulle claimed the empire as theirs, not least because they both needed imperial legitimacy to buttress their claims to represent the 'true' France.

This had direct consequences for the political shape of the French empire. Already by September 1940, the French New Hebrides, most of AEF, New Caledonia and the French territories in India and the Pacific had sworn allegiance to de Gaulle's Free France. They were followed by Syria in 1941 and Madagascar in 1942. By the time the Allies launched the D-Day landings in June 1944, the French empire was an administrative mess. In addition to the territories that had rapidly declared for Free France, others had been retaken by force (this included most of North Africa) or had been lost entirely (as was the case with Indochina, which was occupied by the Japanese in March 1944). It was an indication of the complex nature of the situation

on the ground that, in various places in the Middle
East and elsewhere, Free French and Vichy units –
often made up of colonial soldiers – fought against
each other. No other European colonial power experienced this kind of division of loyalty amongst its
colonial armies.

The war also had profound consequences for those
who lived under colonial rule, a fact that later provided a major impetus for decolonization. In the most
extreme cases, the worst policies of the Vichy state were
enacted in the colonies. Algeria, for example, was the
only part of France in which French Jews were abruptly
stripped of their citizenship when the Vichy government abrogated the 1870 Crémieux Decrees that had
made them French half a century before. Elsewhere,
savage repression by French colonial authorities and
the conscription of thousands of young men to fight
for the French army brought the realities of the war to
isolated villages and communities. The sheer number
of colonial soldiers gives a sense of the scale of imperial involvement in the French war effort. In 1939–40,
approximately 178,000 West and Central Africans and
320,000 North Africans were drafted into the French
army. Of these, almost 43,000 ended up stranded in
metropolitan France as prisoners of war and at least
5,000 deserted to join the Free French armies. Many
colonial soldiers – on both sides – participated in the
battles to liberate France in 1944. It is no exaggeration
to say that France was liberated by and from its colonies. For de Gaulle's Free France, in particular, the

empire was uniquely important since it was the only part of France that could claim not to have been sullied by surrender and occupation.

The centrality of empire to de Gaulle and Free France had fateful consequences since it guaranteed that the colonies would remain firmly French after the war. Notwithstanding the immense difficulties the French state faced in governing a vast and broken empire after the Liberation, it did not for a moment contemplate abandoning its overseas territories, except in the case of the Middle East, where it was largely forced to do so under international pressure. On the contrary, it set about tying them more closely to the metropole. Already in the Brazzaville Declaration of February 1944, de Gaulle and the Free French had ruled out the possibility of any form of independence. Instead, they suggested the creation of a new 'union' that would put an end to the patchwork of different administrations across the French empire. The French Union was duly established as part of the new constitution of the Fourth Republic in 1946. This provided the basis for a supposedly more 'equal' relationship between France's remaining colonies in Africa, Asia, the Caribbean, the Indian Ocean and the Pacific. It introduced limited forms of elected self-government and greater colonial representation in Paris and committed the French state to the economic development of its overseas territories.

But the realities of colonial rule blunted the impact of these idealistic policies. A powerful – and ultimately terminal – anti-colonial insurgency in Indochina in the late 1940s, open revolt in Madagascar in 1947 and the development of organized anti-colonial resistance in Algeria in the 1950s ensured that many of the aims of the French Union were stillborn. Even so, the emergence of local forms of self-government and substantial attempts on the part of the French to 'develop' their empire by force had important effects on local populations. In West Africa, for instance, the experience of politics helped to create an articulate and influential African colonial elite, and a new generation of trade unionists organized ever more powerful protests against colonial rule. Meanwhile, the forced modernization inflicted on Algeria's rural areas resulted in massive population displacement and spiralling urbanization, as workers left the countryside in droves. This process transformed the socioeconomic structure of the region, with long-lasting consequences for the Algerian War and postcolonial relations between France and Algeria.

There was no better example of a project to develop France's colonial possessions than the Constantine Plan of 1958. This was supposed to do for Algeria what a decade of state planning had done in post-war metropolitan France. The aim was to build hundreds of thousands of new houses, redistribute large amounts of rural land, introduce compulsory schooling and gradually bring the salaries of Algerian workers in line with those of their metropolitan French counterparts. The plan even included the introduction of a specific quota for Algerians within the French civil service, a form of affirmative action that would be almost unthinkable in France today. As with the idea of the French Union, however, the realities of colonial rule in Algeria meant that very few of these proposals saw the light of day. By 1958, Algeria was locked into an increasingly violent civil and anti-colonial war, which made the French state's efforts at development appear either farcical or sinister. Nevertheless, the Constantine Plan remains one of the most ambitious development projects ever envisaged by a European colonial power. It demonstrated that, until the bitter end, the French state took its colonial burden seriously, despite overwhelming evidence that its empire was falling apart.

There were many reasons for this French stubbornness, perhaps even denial, in relation to its empire. As we saw earlier, the empire was inextricably linked to the liberation of France during the war. It was not simply that the colonies had supplied up to one quarter of French troops; it was also that the French empire was a necessary part of the Free French narrative of resistance. But the war had another important consequence: it created what some historians describe as a form of 'territorial anxiety'. The humiliation of the fall of France in 1940 was multiplied by the fact that French territory was carved up, given away, occupied or lost during the war. This meant that reclaiming territory was a fundamental aim of the post-war French state. Unlike the British, who more readily moved towards systems of informal control over parts of their empire, the French were obsessed with the physical space of their overseas territories. After 1945, French politicians and military generals repeatedly hammered home the message that there should be no loss of territory.

The results of this policy were most clearly visible in Indochina, where the French state missed a number of opportunities after the war to negotiate an orderly withdrawal in the way that the British did in India and Palestine in 1947. Instead, it decided not only to reclaim the entirety of Indochinese territory after 1945, but also to obliterate Ho Chi Minh's anti-colonial insurgency. Like the Constantine Plan, this was impossibly idealistic. The logistical realities of fighting a colonial war on the other side of the world and the strength of the Vietminh war effort eventually got the better of the French army in 1954. In their attempts to preserve France's status as a colonial power with territory on every continent, the French political and military elites led the country to a catastrophic defeat on the battlefield.

Another reason for France's attachment to its empire can be found in the peculiarities of French colonial ideology. From the early nineteenth century onwards, political elites had justified colonial expansion on the grounds that France had a unique *mission civilisatrice* (civilizing mission). This entailed not simply governing 'lesser' races and peoples, but also raising them to the same level of 'civilization' as white Europeans. In so doing, the colonized would slowly be 'assimilated' into the French nation. The discourse of assimilation was not merely hypocrisy: at various points, certain people who lived in the colonies were given the right to vote, direct representation in the French parliament and full French citizenship. As early as 1792, there was colonial representation in the Assemblée nationale. This was partly re-established after the revolution of 1848 and then more fully with the advent of the Third Republic in 1870. The territorial distribution of this representation and the nature of the electoral franchise were highly inconsistent and unequal until 1946, but the sight of black *députés* in the French parliament in the late nineteenth century was without parallel. No other European colonial power took the idea of assimilation and citizenship as seriously as the French did.

As a result, support for French colonialism was not limited to military generals, outright racists and white settlers. There was also a 'progressive' case for French colonialism that appealed to many parts of the French left. Indeed, after the Second World War, it was a desire to live up to the ideals of assimilation that led progressive administrators and politicians to propose such grandiose initiatives as the Constantine Plan. In hindsight, it is easy to dismiss these projects to 'improve' and 'develop' the French empire as a further example of patronizing French paternalism, foisted on recalcitrant colonized peoples at gunpoint. But many of those who came up with them genuinely believed that they were contributing to a fairer distribution of economic, social and political power.

The problem, of course, was that a progressive vision of colonialism was virtually impossible to sustain in the face of open colonial conflict. During the Algerian War, well-meaning civil servants, nurses and philanthropists soon discovered that their attempts to improve sanitary and living conditions were simultaneously part of a war effort. Under the cover of humanitarian interventions and development projects, the French army and police tried to coerce and cajole Algerians into abandoning the anti-colonial cause or denouncing those who had already joined the liberation movement. The contradiction between the stated progressive aims of development projects and the brutality of counter-insurgency, torture and guerrilla warfare was too great. Even in parts of the French empire that were not engaged in total war, the tension between the myth of assimilation and the reality of racism was painfully obvious to those who lived under colonial rule. By the late 1950s, the *mission civilisatrice* was in tatters, its good intentions buried under a pile of dead bodies.

Given the extreme violence of decolonization in places like Algeria, Indochina and Madagascar, one might assume that the end of empire marked a clean break. But this was not the case. Relations between France and its former colonies persisted long after the end of empire. The French left behind hundreds of millions of French-speakers all over the world, many of whom remained tied to the metropole through migration and postcolonial links. Decolonization created an entire subgroup of people who could claim full French citizenship by descent without ever setting foot in Paris or Marseille. France remained for decades the privileged trading partner for Francophone African countries, and the main source of technical development assistance. And even French politicians were forced to continue attending to the needs of former imperial citizens. One of the more remarkable features of contemporary French politics is the sight of French election polling booths in Casablanca, Nouméa and Chennai, which today are used to elect specific members of parliament for overseas French citizens.

Decolonization also reshaped the politics and society of metropolitan France. From the 1960s onwards, wave upon wave of postcolonial migrants arrived on French shores. Some of these were the sons and daughters of the colonized, such as Algerians, Vietnamese, Moroccans, Malians and many others who travelled to the former colonial metropole in search of better jobs, better education and better salaries. Others were the former colonizers. Almost 1 million European settlers – known as *pieds-noirs* – left Algeria at the end of the war in 1962. This mass exodus was the biggest population movement in post-war Europe and led to the rise of a strong *pied-noir* identity, especially in the southern regions of the Languedoc, the Rhône Valley, the Camargue and the Côte d'Azur. Finally, there were those who fell awkwardly between colonizer and colonized, like the *harkis* – the term given to Algerian auxiliaries who fought in the French army during the Algerian War. Denounced as traitors by the postcolonial Algerian state and ignored by the French in their attempt to forget the painful legacies of decolonization, many *harkis* fled to France at the end of the Algerian War, only to languish for years in former concentration camps in rural areas.

The presence of so many people whose experiences were shaped by the French empire and its demise has inevitably led to protracted, sometimes vitriolic, battles over colonial memory. This has manifested itself in local struggles over street names and memorials, as well as lengthy parliamentary debates about compensation and historical recognition. The *pieds-noirs*, for example, have fought to receive compensation from the French state for the property they lost after the independence of Algeria (they have mostly failed), while anti-colonial activists campaigned for years for slavery to be recognized as a 'crime against humanity' (this eventually became law in 2001). In a similar vein, there have been prickly public debates since the 1990s about whether France should 'apologize' for colonialism, with some arguing for such a gesture as a moral imperative, and others dismissing it as little more than the latest instance of a pernicious culture of 'repentance'. Just like the conflicting stories of defeat and resistance during the Second World War, these postcolonial *guerres de mémoires* (memory wars) have acted as incessant reminders of the degree to which the past remains tangled up with the present.

But France's colonial legacy in the twenty-first century does not only take the form of memory struggles; it lives on in a much more concrete form in the parts of the French empire that were never decolonized at all. Almost every European colonial power has vestiges of empire in the form of small, isolated islands, but France still governs more than 2.8 million people in Guadeloupe, Martinique, French Guiana, French Polynesia, New Caledonia, Mayotte and Réunion. These highly diverse territories are inhabited by French citizens, are tied to France politically and act as a major drain on the state's resources. They are a living, evolving piece of France's colonial heritage. They capture the idealism of the colonial project through the enduring power of the French language and French culture, to which many of their inhabitants are genuinely attached. But they also embody its most disturbing elements, from the multi-generational violence of slavery in the Caribbean to the ambiguities of settler colonialism in New Caledonia. Often ignored or dismissed as 'peripheral' parts of France, these territories encapsulate the ongoing contradictions of French colonialism.

## The Promise of Anti-Colonialism

Anti-colonialism is inseparable from – and as old as – colonialism itself. In the French case, the modern history of anti-colonialism begins, like so many other things, with the French Revolution. It was in the period after 1789 that the key paradox of French anti-colonialism took shape, namely how to realize the emancipatory, universalist and egalitarian potential of the French Revolution within a colonial reality of servitude, difference and hierarchy. Over the next two centuries, anti-colonial activists in the Francophone world returned incessantly to this paradox, and it formed the basis of some of the most bitter conflicts between colonizer and colonized.

Broadly speaking, there have been three responses to the post-revolutionary paradox of French anti-colonialism. The first can be described as ethical or humanist anti-colonialism. This has emphasized the mistreatment of indigenous peoples and has urged colonial authorities to treat the colonized with 'respect'. This discourse was popular with abolitionists in the nineteenth century and young white anti-colonial activists in the 1950s, and it remains present today in the legacy of international development aid. The second is economic anti-colonialism, which took on increasingly Marxist or communist overtones in the twentieth century. This was the stock-in-trade of nationalist leaders who led their countries to independence and has continued in contemporary anti-globalization rhetoric surrounding neo-colonialism. Finally, there is a culturalist form of anti-colonialism, articulated around the characteristics of racial, ethnic or cultural groups. The most famous example of this was the artistic movement known as *négritude*, but it has made a reappearance in recent decades around civil rights campaigns for Muslims, blacks and other ethnic minority populations.

All three of these strands have their own pre-revolutionary genealogies, but they came together in spectacular fashion in the Haitian Revolution (1791–1804), easily the most important moment of anti-colonial theory and practice in the French empire after 1789. Like its metropolitan French counterpart, the Haitian Revolution was a vast and complex conflict, pitting different racialized communities against a variety of colonial forces. During the course of the Revolution, the inhabitants of Haiti – formerly known as Saint Domingue – were exposed to every kind of colonial and anti-colonial thinking, from the intransigent pro-colonialism of the terrified French planters to the ethical abolitionism of the white French governor Léger-Félicité Sonthonax, who first proclaimed the end of slavery on the island in 1793. They were also confronted with the strident black anti-colonialism of Toussaint Louverture, and the authoritarian zeal of his successor Jean-Jacques Dessalines. In a short space of time, Haiti became a veritable laboratory for anti-colonial ideas and an inspiration to anti-colonial activists across the world.

Unfortunately, the century or so following the Haitian Revolution was not a propitious time for anti-colonial thought. Despite the huge influence of its revolution, Haiti itself sank into a prolonged period of political stagnation and economic decline. Various forms of ethical anti-colonialism made some progress; slavery was definitively abolished during the revolution of 1848 and some very select colonial citizens were given the right to vote. But these were often little more than symbolic attempts at rectifying the injustice of colonialism. The harsh truth was that the nineteenth century was a period of intensive and brutal colonial expansion. Vastly superior firepower ensured that there was little effective resistance to colonial rule, while anthropological theories of racial superiority and a firm belief in the *mission civilisatrice* meant that anti-colonial ideas were all but inaudible.

Two global events put an end to this period of relative quiescence: the First World War and the Russian Revolution of 1917. The former drew millions of colonial soldiers into European armies. This forced colonial administrators to reckon with a large number of indigenous people who had paid a 'blood debt' to their colonial masters and expected due recompense. The latter signalled the triumph of a radical new philosophy of emancipation – communism – which had the potential to transform the world order. It is hardly surprising, then, that the interwar period was the second major anti-colonial moment in modern French history after the revolutionary period of the late eighteenth century. Throughout the 1920s and 1930s, bright young activists from across the French empire crossed paths in Paris – an 'anti-imperial metropolis', in the words of the historian Michael

Goebel – in search of solutions to the ever-worsening social, economic and cultural conditions in France's colonies.

This flourishing of anti-colonial ideas in interwar France had important consequences for the post-war period. For a start, several of the most famous anti-colonial and revolutionary leaders of the 1940s and 1950s were educated in Paris, including Ho Chi Minh, Zhou Enlai and Deng Xiaoping. Interwar France was also the crucible of the *négritude* movement. This variant of anti-colonialism, which blended a culturalist critique of racism and an economic critique of imperialism, came about because of the encounter between three black students in Paris in the late 1920s: Aimé Césaire from Martinique, Léon Gontran Damas from French Guiana and Léopold Sédar Senghor from Senegal. Inspired by the Harlem Renaissance, global communism and France's own radical traditions such as symbolist poetry and the Haitian Revolution, they created a movement that sought to reclaim and emancipate black peoples through art and politics.

After the Second World War, the three founding fathers of *négritude* engaged directly in electoral politics. Damas served briefly as a *député* for French Guiana from 1948 to 1951, while Césaire and Senghor became two of the longest-serving politicians in the Francophone world. Césaire was mayor of Fort-de-France continuously from 1945 until 2001 and *député* for Martinique from 1945 until 1993. Senghor was a *député* from Senegal from 1945 until 1958, and then ruled independent Senegal from 1960 until 1980. Césaire was initially elected as a Communist, before leaving the party in dramatic fashion in 1956 after writing a famous letter to the then leader, Maurice Thorez, denouncing the narrowness of class politics. Senghor was elected as a socialist within the Section française de l'internationale ouvrière (SFIO, French Section of the Workers' International), before leaving in the early 1950s to set up his own socialist movement in Senegal. Both Senghor and Césaire became political figures of extraordinary prestige in their native lands.

While anti-colonial activism during the 1930s and 1940s was characterized by an emerging articulation of the radical injustice of French colonialism, there was little consensus on the preferred political solution. Full independence was often not the main demand of anti-colonial movements and their leaders, even as late as the 1950s. Many believed that the wrongs of colonialism could be rectified by a process of tighter integration between France and its colonies. They argued that the extension of civil, political and economic rights to colonized peoples was more important than self-determination. A good example of this position was Césaire. In 1945, he argued for the benefits of integration and called – successfully – for Martinique to be granted the formal status of a *département*. For him, as for other members of the colonial elite in this period, the point of anti-colonialism was to allow the colonized to have the same opportunities as those afforded to their European rulers. Complete political independence was not a necessary step to achieving this goal.

The problem was that the wrongs of colonialism were inherent in colonialism itself. There were moments after the end of the Second World War when it seemed possible that substantial reforms might take place across the French empire, but these promises either evaporated or turned sour. The violence of the conflicts in Indochina and Algeria, and a growing anger amongst a younger generation of scholars, activists and political leaders, made dreams of 'unity' and 'federation' appear hopelessly outdated. Even Césaire had mostly embraced the cause of independence by the time the Algerian War was over. With the advent of the Cuban Revolution in 1959, the ethical anti-colonialism of colonial reformers and the utopian aesthetic revolt of the *négritude* movement began to be definitively outflanked by an anti-colonialism of independence and self-determination. The colonial soldiers who had fought in the Second World War could readily draw parallels between the evils of fascism and the evils of colonialism. In the French case specifically, the irony was all the more poignant because the soldiers and generals sent to put down unrest in Indochina and Algeria often did so in the name of 'resistance' and claimed they were restoring France's place in the world after the Nazi occupation. This eerie dialogue of the deaf – in which anti-colonial activists and French generals both claimed the mantle of the French Resistance – was famously staged in Gillo Pontecorvo's epoch-defining film *The Battle of Algiers* (1966), which recounted the vicious suppression of the popular uprising against French rule in Algiers in 1957.

The inspiration behind Pontecorvo's film was one of the most emblematic intellectuals of this third anti-colonial moment: Frantz Fanon. Born in Martinique, Fanon was another extremely gifted product of the French colonial education system. Having been taught by Césaire in the early 1940s, Fanon was initially drawn towards *négritude*. But his post-war higher education in metropolitan France exposed him to the strident communism of 1950s France and the history of psychoanalysis. These diverse influences filtered through into his two best-known texts: *Peau noire, masques blancs* (*Black Skin, White Masks*, 1952) and *Les damnés de la terre* (*The Wretched of the Earth*, 1961). The first dealt directly with the dialectical relationship between blacks and whites – their hostility towards each other, their dependence on each other and the inability of blacks to express themselves except through the language and ideas of whiteness. The second, which became one of the great texts of the global anti-colonial movement, drew on the same dialectical model, but extended the analysis to colonialism in its entirety.

By this time, Fanon had worked at the psychiatric hospital of Blida-Joinville in the mid-1950s, before becoming directly involved in the struggle for Algerian independence. This first-hand experience of the colonial endgame in North Africa – and the fact that he had terminal leukaemia when he composed the text – gave *Les damnés de la terre* an urgent, tragic quality. While most readers have been drawn towards the (in)famous opening chapter, which endorses violence as a rational and cathartic response to the historic violence of colonialism, the latter parts of the book are more ambiguous. Fanon was acutely aware of the devastating psychological effects of war on all sides and he expressed concerns about the potential for authoritarian postcolonial nationalisms. Sadly, he died a few days before the book was published and several months before Algeria officially gained its independence. But his intense and contradictory ideas encapsulated perfectly the thrust of Francophone anti-colonial thought in the 1950s and 1960s. Fanon, in common with other anti-colonial intellectuals like Albert Memmi, believed history had finally turned its back on colonialism.

One of the more unusual aspects about anti-colonialism during the post-war period was the wide support it received from metropolitan activists and intellectuals. Famous figures like Jean-Paul Sartre, Simone de Beauvoir and Gisèle Halimi denounced French colonial rule, but so too did thousands of students and activists, who were horrified by the violence of decolonization. Of the many issues that galvanized anti-colonial sentiment, the most important was undoubtedly the revelation of torture by the

French army. It was Henri Alleg's celebrated pamphlet *La question* (1958) that brought the issue to wide public attention. His graphic descriptions of the waterboarding and electric shocks he endured confirmed long-standing suspicions about the barbarity of colonial war. After selling 60,000 copies in a matter of weeks, *La question* was banned by the French authorities. But it was not enough to silence those who believed that the French state had failed to abide by the most elementary rules of war. It is an indication of the depth of unease provoked by the issue that, when General Paul Aussaresses frankly acknowledged the existence of torture during the Algerian War in an incendiary memoir published in 2001, the public outcry was almost as intense as it had been in the late 1950s.

For the overwhelming majority of anti-colonial activists, the end of the French colonial empire in the 1960s was a source of immense satisfaction. Even where the unravelling of the colonial project resulted in outright civil war – as in Algeria – the formal departure of the French was celebrated as an unambiguous victory for colonized peoples. But the end of empire did not mean the end of anti-colonial politics. On the contrary, anti-colonialism in the post-colonial Francophone world continued to be divided along roughly the same lines as in earlier periods. The ethical anti-colonialism of the nineteenth century, for example, was plainly visible in the plethora of French international aid projects and charities. The

prominent role of French NGOs like Médecins sans
frontières (founded in 1971) renewed the tradition of
sympathetic external – mostly white – concern about
the plight of those living in the ex-colonial world.
Closer to home, there were countless campaigns
against police violence towards ethnic minorities in
metropolitan France, from the 1983 Marche pour
l'égalité et contre le racisme (March for Equality and
against Racism) to the ongoing protests against the
death of 24-year-old Adama Traoré in police custody
in 2016. These campaigns mobilized a new generation of activists in an attempt to stamp out the institutional legacies of racism and colonialism.

Likewise, the Marxist-inspired anti-colonialism of
the late-colonial period was reconfigured in all sorts
of ways for the postcolonial landscape. Within the
French left, for example, solidarity with anti-colonial
and revolutionary struggles in the 'Third World' was
central to the emergence of the French New Left in
the 1960s and 1970s. This shift was an important
impetus for the formation of a new left-wing party –
the Parti socialiste (PS) – in the 1970s. At the same
time, anti-colonialism became official state ideology
in former colonies after decolonization. This meant
that everyone from ailing dictators to famous musi-
cians made a point of condemning France as a rapa-
cious and manipulative neo-colonial power. This did
not require a great deal of imagination. The knowledge that French intelligence services were interven-
ing in the governance of West African countries, that

French firms were monopolizing oil extraction in the Sahara Desert and that the French state was conducting nuclear testing in the South Pacific made it seem as if colonialism had never really ended.

Finally, there has been a resurgence of identity-based anti-colonialism since the 2000s. As we will see, the contemporary French state is extremely reluctant to acknowledge ethnic, religious and cultural difference for fear that this will lead to the unravelling of the unity of the French nation. But this has come under sustained attack from a growing constellation of ethnic minority pressure groups and cultural organizations. At the more political end of the spectrum, groups like the Indigènes de la République have attempted to combine anti-colonialism and a pungent critique of contemporary French republicanism. In a less obviously political vein, African music festivals, major cultural venues like the Institut du monde arabe in Paris and organizations dedicated to advancing ethnic minority employees in the private sector have all contributed to a renewed interest in different forms of identity politics. Along with the penetration of Anglophone postcolonial thought into the French academy and the influence of American identity politics on activist organizations, it is now possible – if still highly controversial – for people to articulate anti-colonial positions through the prism of 'Islam', 'decoloniality' and 'blackness'. Not since the days of *négritude* has there been such a clear politicization of identity in the realm of anti-colonial activism.

It is tempting to see some of this anti-colonial activism as just another example of the use of the past for political polemic. This may be true in some cases. But, if anti-colonialism persists as a powerful language of politics, it is mostly because it tells a different history of France and its empire, one that is littered with broken promises, inequality and violence. This makes for a powerful counter-narrative to the erstwhile hubris of the *mission civilisatrice*. Today, a curious young activist in the Francophone world can engage with anti-colonialism in the canonical works of thinkers like Césaire and Fanon and in the reggae songs of Ivoirian singer Tiken Jah Fakoly, the cultured hip-hop of MC Solaar or the fiction of Guadeloupean author Maryse Condé. For all of these artists, anti-colonialism not only has something to say about contemporary injustice, it also draws on a lineage that stretches through the Algerian War and the interwar struggle for colonial justice, all the way back to the slave revolts in Saint Domingue. This proud tradition – and the fact that colonialism and its legacy remain urgent public issues today – should ensure that anti-colonialism continues to flourish for many years to come.

# 3

# Grandeur and Decline

In France, the term 'grandeur' is inextricably associated with the presidency of Charles de Gaulle, which ran from 1958 to 1969. During this period, a rejuvenated and rebuilt France inspired its citizens. The privations of the immediate post-war years gave way to a booming economy, high growth rates, very low unemployment and far-reaching social transformation. On the global stage, France was no longer a country that lived in the shadow of Nazi occupation and colonial calamity. Instead, de Gaulle led a robust foreign policy that appeared to make France a key broker in the Cold War. The development of an independent arsenal of nuclear weapons and a network of nuclear power stations symbolized a nation at the cutting edge of technological and military innovation. France was once again a great power, and the French people knew it.

True to his talents as a politician, de Gaulle took a lot of the credit for this success. But the origins of France's post-war economic growth, commonly known as the 'Trente Glorieuses', lay in the extraordinary state-led transformation of society in the decades following the end of the war. As was the case in many other parts of Europe in the late 1940s and 1950s, the state played a central role in steering a shattered continent back to health. In Western Europe, vigorous state investment led to the construction of new health services, sophisticated social security systems and vast transport infrastructures. In Eastern Europe, the heavy hand of the communist state did much the same thing, bringing industrialization, urbanization and social services to regions that had been devastated by the brutal war on the Eastern Front. On paper, Cold War Europe was irreconcilably divided by ideology from the late 1940s onwards, but, in practice, the forms of state intervention that were implemented in Paris resembled those implemented in Poznań, Prague and Pisa.

### The Road to Grandeur: France's Long Reconstruction

Given the importance of the state in French history, all the way back to the *ancien régime*, it is hardly surprising that France became a paradigmatic case of reconstruction. Nowhere else in Western Europe did post-war reconstruction simultaneously imply such a profound degree of social and economic transformation. This began at the very top. In 1946, de Gaulle set up the Commissariat général du Plan (CGP). This agency – which would not have been out of place in a communist regime in Eastern Europe – was supposed to be the key agent of central planning. The CGP was in charge of setting macroeconomic priorities across a range of sectors in the form of five-year plans. Its inaugural director was Jean Monnet, later one of the architects of European integration. The first five-year plan was announced in 1946; the second in 1954. Together, these represented a major attempt to steer crucial sectors of the economy, including mining, agriculture, transport and steel. The remit of the second plan was also extended to include many public services. It was a testament to the importance of central planning that it continued until 1993, despite a rejection of the ideology of state planning across the Western world from the mid-1970s onwards.

For civil servants, the aim of central planning was to give direction to socio-economic processes that were already happening. It was designed to ensure economic development could be managed across metropolitan France and, in some cases, the French empire as well. But these aspirations would have been stillborn had it not been for some important geopolitical changes. For a start, France received more than 2 billion US dollars of Marshall aid from 1947 to 1951 – more funds than any other country. This was supplemented by rapidly growing foreign direct investment, especially by American firms. Multinational corporations like Coca-Cola and Caterpillar became far more prominent after the Second World War, as they looked to expand into new markets. These visible – and sometimes unpopular – inputs of foreign cash and investment contributed to strong growth rates in the 1950s. In the first half of the twentieth century, economists had continuously worried that the French economy lagged behind those of its competitors, but suddenly it was expanding faster than ever. By the 1950s, the country's notoriously traditional agricultural sector was modernizing rapidly, and industrial production had taken off.

The French economy also benefited from increasingly successful attempts to manage the Franco-German border after the war. The French adopted multiple strategies to solve a border problem that had caused repeated – and costly – military confrontations. The first of these was to secure German territory. When the joint Allied occupation of Germany ended in 1949, the French refused to cede the Saarland. Instead, this small area to the east of the Rhine river was, like Morocco and Tunisia, converted into a French protectorate and governed in this way until 1957. This ensured complete French control of the region. The second strategy involved the creation of a common market for coal and steel along the Rhine, which was formally inaugurated as the European Coal and Steel Community (ECSC) in 1951. This became the precursor to the European Economic Community (EEC), the European Community (EC) and the European Union (EU). Even though the treaty that brought the ECSC into being was ratified by five other countries – Belgium, Italy, Luxembourg, the Netherlands and West Germany – the main beneficiary was France. Behind a diplomatic language that stressed peace and prosperity, the main function of the ECSC was to secure French access to the valuable coal fields of the

Ruhr, thereby guaranteeing French jurisdiction over a resource that had been used to supercharge the Nazi war effort only a few years before.

Central planning, substantial inward investment and relative stability along the Franco-German border provided the macroeconomic framework for France's post-war boom. But these were accompanied by vast changes in the structure and geography of French society. While urbanization and industrialization were common features of post-war economic development everywhere in Europe, the effect of these processes was greater in France than elsewhere. Compared to the United Kingdom and Germany, France was a more rural and agricultural society in the interwar period. Even in 1950, the agricultural sector made up more than 10% of the gross national product, and the importance of agriculture was reaffirmed in the early negotiations around the EEC in the late 1950s, which led to the creation of the Common Agricultural Policy. As the American scholar Laurence Wylie discovered when he took his family to live in a small village in southern France in 1950, the French were still powerfully rooted to the land and deeply committed to an idea of *terroir* (literally, 'earth').

On his return to the United States, Wylie wrote a famous anthropological study about his experiences, entitled *Village in the Vaucluse* (1957). It was a moving account of a rural community, almost frozen in time, touched only in the most superficial ways by the rhetoric and reality of the post-war boom. He described old men in flat caps drinking in the village bar, absorbed in family struggles over land and property, and young people who could not imagine moving more than a few kilometres from the place they were born. The book quickly became a classic, but today's readers find it hard to square Wylie's description of a static rural world with the relentless modernity of twenty-first-century France, with its glistening high-speed trains and avant-garde architecture. This is because the very fabric of French society was reshaped in the decades after Wylie's first visit. Older ideas of *terroir* have not disappeared, but they were substantially remodelled by the social transformations that took place during the 'Trente Glorieuses'.

One of the most important ways in which French society changed was through greater mobility. In the 1950s and 1960s, car ownership exploded, opening new horizons to the country's rural populations. A shiny new network of trunk roads (*routes nationales*) and, from 1960 onwards, motorways (*autoroutes*) offered new possibilities for work and leisure. The penetration of other consumer goods had a similar transformative impact. The huge increase in the number of refrigerators changed the way people stored food and led to the rise of the *hypermarché* (large supermarket), where people could do substantial shops, ideally using their new cars. Contrary to the popular perception of France as a land of small shopkeepers, the French were pioneers in supermarket culture. Several of the most famous supermarket chains opened their first stores in the post-war decades, including E. Leclerc in 1949, Carrefour in 1959 and Auchan in 1961. These were ideal places for aspirational French people to spend their hard-earned cash.

Part of the reason for this growing disposable income was an abrupt shift in patterns of class stratification. In 1945, the heads of 45% of French households were independent workers, who lived by running a small farm, business or shop; by 1985, 85% of the population were wage earners, with a substantial proportion (20%) working as managers (*cadres*). Elsewhere, industrial expansion – which was especially noticeable between 1950 and 1965 – drew millions of workers to towns and cities. In 1946, around 50% of the population lived in urban areas; in 1975, this had risen to 68%. This in-migration swelled the ranks of the industrial proletariat. Indeed, most scholars would agree that the post-war decades were the apogee of working-class culture in France, with strong local community networks, and substantial political representation in the form of the PCF and its affiliated trade union, the Confédération générale du travail (CGT, General Confederation of Labour). These sectoral changes in the French economy, and impressive growth rates of almost 5% a year through the 1950s and 1960s, led to very low rates of unemployment of less than 2%. This was all the more remarkable considering that this was also a period when rates of foreign immigration increased rapidly. For a brief period, there were enough jobs to absorb both an influx of foreign workers and the internal displacement caused by the profound changes in the structure of the French economy.

As far as France's planners were concerned, these developments were overwhelmingly positive. High birth rates, urbanization, industrialization, high levels of immigration and the spread of consumer products indicated that France was on the path to modernization. But planners were not simply concerned with making people work harder; they also wanted the state to do more. They embarked on a series of projects designed to protect, look after and house the French. Already at the time of the Liberation, the Conseil national de la Résistance had grand plans for introducing a comprehensive social security system that would do away with the patchwork of state legislation and employer schemes that had existed before. In many respects, this plan did eventually come to fruition, especially in the realm of family policy. The post-war French state introduced some of the most generous child subsidies (*allocations familiales*) and maternity benefits in Europe as a way of encouraging the demographic boom. It also vastly expanded state-subsidized social health insurance, which became available to 20 million employees by the late 1940s, up from 7 million in 1944. Despite their statist leanings, French technocrats never attempted to create a health system of the scale and complexity of the British National Health Service; this would have been too costly and would have required curtailing too many vested interests in the medical profession. Nevertheless, the expansion of family policy and social security was almost universally popular amongst the electorate and they remain core elements of the French welfare system today.

Another area in which the state intervened on a large scale was in the domain of housing. During the Second World War, one in twenty buildings were destroyed and one in five were damaged, leaving millions of people displaced from their homes (as late as 1946, there were still 640,000 people living in hotels). This made the physical reconstruction of the urban environment a political priority. Even though it was not until the early 1950s that the French state began to execute its ambitious plans to house a growing population, the progress after that was undeniable. More than 7 million new housing units were constructed by the French state between 1951 and 1974, with over 2 million of these in the form of *habitations à loyer modéré* (HLM or low-rent social housing). Entire neighbourhoods burst out of the countryside on the outskirts of French cities, most of which were conceived according to rational modernist principles. Carefully designed apartments in large tower blocks were designed to provide the best possible living environment at a reasonable cost. In many cases, those who took up residence in these areas benefited from modern conveniences like indoor toilets or central heating to which they had never had access. In their early years, these new neighbourhoods – some of which, like Sarcelles on the northern outskirts of Paris or the so-called *quartiers nord* of Marseille, have since developed fearsome reputations – were hailed as a triumph of successful state planning. It seemed that the state had finally found a way to house its people and satisfy their growing demands for comfort.

The peak of France's post-war social and economic boom was around 1965. Economic growth continued to rise until the sharp slowdown of the mid-1970s, but it was in the mid-1960s that the country's 'long reconstruction' – to use the historian Herrick Chapman's formulation – finally came to an end. Seen in retrospect, the mid-1960s appear as a moment of relative political stability, social cohesion and global prestige. They are also closely associated with the leadership of de Gaulle. He was the person who presided over the renaissance of his beloved France and it was his authority that held together a fragile political and economic order. De Gaulle had peremptorily 'retired' from public life in 1946, largely because his political vision had been marginalized with the return of parliamentary politics. But the acute crisis of the Fourth Republic, precipitated by the spiralling costs of France's colonial wars, set the stage for his return. After being invited in May 1958 to form a government of national unity, de Gaulle set about taking advantage of the unique circumstances to reshape French politics in his image.

He began by drafting a new constitution, which was duly approved in a referendum in September 1958. This marked the beginning of the Fifth Republic, which de Gaulle saw as the first step in shoring up the country's supposedly weak and fractious political institutions. A few years later in 1962, he would go one step further by creating the directly elected presidency, a constitutional change that fitted with his vision of a strong executive that could rise above the political fray. His next task was to negotiate a withdrawal from Algeria, which required an extraordinary degree of political dexterity. On the one hand, de Gaulle had always insisted on France's civilizing mission and the importance of the French empire; on the other hand, he realized that, without solving the Algerian crisis, there was no way of restoring national unity. He was thus fighting a war on three fronts: against radicalized Algerian nationalists; against angry European settlers (who were bitterly opposed to independence and even organized an abortive putsch in April 1961 to wrest control of Algeria); and against a French electorate exhausted by a murderous colonial war.

In hindsight, the withdrawal from Algeria in March 1962 appears inevitable, but it still had to be sold to the French people as something other than a defeat. Only de Gaulle could have achieved this. Even though Algeria had formally been considered an integral part of France for decades, de Gaulle quickly modified the story of French colonization to make it sound as if the loss of Algeria was a result of a profound incompatibility between France and the Arabo-Muslim world. This allowed him to dismiss as anachronistic the recriminations of European settlers – the so-called *pieds-noirs* – who accused him of betraying them. It also allowed him to present the end of the Algerian War as a necessary step for the restoration of national unity. By executing this balancing act, not only did de Gaulle become the saviour of France once again, he also averted civil war. This did not mean that everyone accepted de Gaulle's authority. For the *pieds-noirs* and for many of the military high command, he was (and still is) an object of hatred for having broken his promise to ensure Algeria would remain forever French. And, from a completely different perspective, many on the left saw his return as an undemocratic power grab by a dictator-in-waiting. Nevertheless, he was the uncontested leader of France by the mid-1960s. His seemingly uncanny ability to appear to the French in their hour of need – whether in 1940, 1944 or 1958 – inspired awe and adulation in equal measure. It seemed only natural that he should be the one to preside over a decade that saw the culmination of a collective reconstruction project, even if the foundations of this project lay in the technocratic state of the much-maligned Fourth Republic.

As the architect of the Fifth Republic, de Gaulle still casts a long shadow over French politics. Every president after him has tried to emulate his seductive combination of messianism, paternalism and authority, but none has really succeeded. This is partly because the socio-economic climate changed radically from the 1970s, but it is also because no president has had the same sense of historical destiny. De Gaulle believed that he was born to lead France and that, if he was given time to reshape the country in his image, it would exude what he called 'grandeur'. For much of the 1960s, he convinced many people that he had succeeded. He was able to initiate grand projects – above all, an ambitious civil and military nuclear programme – and make bold geopolitical moves such as withdrawing from NATO High Command in 1966 without affecting his or his country's prestige. Indeed, a characteristic feature of de Gaulle's foreign policy was to make France seem like a more important player on the world stage than it actually was. In reality, neither Washington nor Moscow cared much what de Gaulle was doing, but he persuaded the French electorate that he had a hotline to both Cold War superpowers. For a country that had, since the nineteenth century, worried about its decadence and decline, the high years of de Gaulle's presidency were a breath of fresh air. Under his watchful eye, the French could, for a brief moment, be proud of their Frenchness.

### The Fear of Decline

The end of de Gaulle's presidency was entirely in keeping with his penchant for dramatic gestures. In 1969, he called a referendum. This was his pre-ferred means of asking the French what they wanted because it did not involve the meddling of parliament. The subject was the decentralization of the

French state, an issue that had become increasingly important in recent years. As a way of raising the stakes, he announced that he would resign immediately if the proposal was not approved. When 52.4% of voters rejected his plans, he promptly retired from politics for a second time. His departure left a gaping void at the heart of French politics, which was only made more acute by his sudden death in November 1970. After such a long period under the tutelage of 'the General', the French were understandably disorientated. The hundreds of thousands of people who gathered for his funeral were saying goodbye both to a great leader and – in de Gaulle's famous words – to 'a certain idea of France'. The future without him was an uncertain one.

The death of de Gaulle was not the only recent event that indicated a society stretched to breaking point. In 1968, a series of student protests in Paris led to one of the largest social movements in modern French history. This brought the country to a standstill and, in the minds of some, to the brink of another political crisis. The *événements de mai 68*, as they became known, put a different gloss on the boom years. They brought to the fore the many people who were anxious about rapid social change and resented the hierarchical state structures that had done so much to promote economic growth. They also stirred up uncomfortable memories of latent authoritarian tendencies and wartime collaboration. In contrast to the shiny new world of advertising and mass consumption, the multi-faceted protests of 1968 showed a darker side to France's post-war boom.

In the French and foreign popular imagination, 1968 is often reduced to a student-led and carnivalesque simulation of left-wing revolutionary politics. Stock images include angry young people manning barricades on the Boulevard Saint-Michel in Paris, and evocative posters created by art school students, with slogans such as 'sous les pavés, la plage!' ('under the paving stones, the beach!'). These stereotypes are not entirely inaccurate. Students were the spark that ignited the protests, and the overwhelming majority of protesters identified with various forms of left-wing politics. The use of powerful imagery and catchy slogans was also a vital part of the power of 1968. For protesters, the aim of their movement was to make the French think differently about the society they lived in. For that, they needed arresting images to shake the bourgeoisie from its torpor.

But the protests of 1968 went much deeper than simply a group of students engaged in revolutionary play-acting. The explosion of radical politics in the mid-1960s reflected broader shifts in French society. A good example of this was the importance of changing gender roles. As early as 1965, the focus of much student activism in Paris was the rigid separation between male and female dorms. In May 1967, male students at the Nanterre campus of the University of Paris staged a sit-in in a female dorm. They argued that the segregation of student accommodation was another example of the rigid hierarchies that dominated French society and the contempt with which young people were treated. Another theme that came up frequently was the quality of student housing. It is no coincidence that Nanterre was one of the most prominent sites of student protest in Paris before 1968. The new Nanterre campus, which was inaugurated in the mid-1960s, was conceived as a response to the huge expansion of higher education. Massive infrastructural investment of this kind was supposed to represent the modernization of French universities. The problem was that planners followed the same modernist principles in the construction of new campuses as they had in the construction of other public housing. The result was that thousands of students found themselves marooned in soulless, concrete buildings on the outskirts of Paris. Worse still, they were within walking distance of one of the most notorious *bidonvilles* (slums) in the city, populated by destitute immigrants from southern Europe and France's former colonies. Students at Nanterre did not need to be told about the gap between the rhetoric of economic growth and the misery of the *bidonville*; they could quite literally see it from the windows of their dorm rooms.

Students were not the only ones to notice that the post-war boom had left many conservative attitudes and social hierarchies intact. Although 1968 is mostly remembered as a conglomeration of student movements, it was also a major moment of labour mobilization. The student protests led to a general strike on 13 May, which was followed by weeks of spontaneous industrial unrest across the country. Inspired by the actions of students – but almost never led by them – large swathes of the skilled workforce walked out of their places of work. At the height of the strike, 10 million people were on strike or unable to work. Factories closed entirely or were run by self-managed workers' groups. For a brief moment, the French successfully upturned the most pervasive hierarchy of all, the distinction between 'boss' and 'worker'. The main trade unions, initially caught completely off-guard by the strikes, slowly tried to gain control of the movement, but they never fully succeeded. Eventually, the protests petered out. By mid-June, few workers were still on strike and the trade unions had secured major concessions from the state. But 1968 still stands as one of the largest worker mobilizations in modern French history.

The involvement of workers in 1968 was vital because it guaranteed the long-term impact of the protests. If these had been limited to Parisian students, they would have been spectacular but superficial. Instead, with the participation of millions of ordinary French people from Brittany to Provence, 1968 became a mass contestation of the established order. Historians estimate that there were at least 1,070 different protests across the country in May and June 1968. These unleashed passionate discussions, organizational enthusiasm and political energy on a scale unseen since the Liberation in 1944. They forced a range of new questions on to the agenda, from the role of women in society and France's relationship to the Catholic Church, to a reassessment of the Vichy past and a growing scepticism about class hierarchies. In some cases, this took a very personalized form, for example in the open attacks on de Gaulle and Gaullist symbols. In other cases, it started a more generalized process, which many people called 'libérer la parole' ('freeing up speech'). The *événements* of 1968 made it possible to talk about some of the social problems that persisted underneath the veneer of economic growth, and they durably broke the ideological stranglehold of the technocratic state.

Not that these long-term consequences were immediately visible. Quite the opposite: the legislative elections that were held in June 1968 as a direct result of the protests returned a crushing victory for the Gaullist party, the Union pour la défense de la République (UDR, Union for the Defence of the Republic). Never before had the right had such a large majority in parliament. But de Gaulle's defeat in the referendum the following year showed that his authority – and that of his allies – was only partially restored. Over the course of the 1970s, the decomposition of the political landscape continued. The liberal Valéry Giscard d'Estaing was elected to the presidency in 1974, and he tried to channel some of the discontent of 1968 in his reforms. He reduced the voting age to 18 – a major demand of student protesters – and pushed through highly controversial changes to women's rights, including the legalization of abortion and divorce by mutual consent. He also deregulated French television and radio, thereby responding to the claim that the media was merely an instrument of the state, another of the prominent battle cries of 1968. The true political heir to 1968, however, was the new Parti socialiste (Socialist Party, PS) founded in 1971. This broad coalition of non-communist left-wing movements – ranging from disgruntled Trotskyists to conservative social democrats – became the *de facto* political home for many former *soixante-huitards* (1968ers). When the party came to power in 1981 under the leadership of François Mitterrand, it continued to implement many of the ideas that had come to prominence in 1968, including the abolition of the death penalty, more favourable treatment of immigrants and substantial investment in public culture.

The long-term legacy of the protests of 1968 was coloured by another – arguably more important – reality: the economic slowdown of the 1970s. The collapse of the Bretton Woods currency exchange system in 1971 and the first oil shock of 1973 brought the golden years of economic growth to an abrupt end. Growth rates plummeted from more than 5% per year in the late 1960s to 1–2% per year in the early 1980s. This brought about a spiralling public deficit as the state's tax receipts dried up. Planners who had got used to stimulating the economy with public money suddenly found that their projections were hopelessly optimistic, and they had no money left to spend. While it was possible to brush off 1968 as the angry posturing of an ungrateful generation, the winds of economic change struck at the very heart of French state power.

Of all the economic transformations that took place in the 1970s, the one that had the most corrosive effect was unemployment. For the three decades following the end of the war, neither the French people nor the French state worried about jobs; there were plenty to go around and wages increased accordingly. This situation changed in the late 1970s. For the first time in 1975, more than a million people were unemployed, the equivalent of 4.8% of the working population. Ten years later, in 1985, the number had risen to 2.6 million. This represented a staggering 10.9% of the workforce. In less than a generation, hundreds of thousands of French people were thrown out of work or unable to find a job. Still today, unemployment remains the scourge of the French economy. Since 1981, the unemployment rate has scarcely dropped below 8% – it was 8.4% in 2019 – and none of the state interventions designed to shore up the labour market has worked. Right-wing policies such as the loosening of labour laws have led mainly to the growth in insecure contracts, while left-wing policies such as the 35-hour working week have failed to create more jobs. In recent years, France has had a dynamic, growing economy, with some of the highest productivity rates in Europe, but the spectre of unemployment is never far away.

The persistence of unemployment in France has exacerbated other dysfunctional aspects of the French labour market. One issue that has become acute in the last decade or two is the sharp distinction between those on permanent contracts (*contrat à durée indéterminée*, CDI), who benefit from generous workers' protection and significant social benefits, and those employed on temporary or part-time contracts. Foreign stereotypes about French workers who take two months of holiday and retire at age 60 do not apply today to the millions of workers who do not have permanent contracts. Another issue is education. In France, there is a long tradition of professional training. Applicants for almost all skilled jobs – from tour guides to train drivers – are expected to have specific qualifications for the job for which they are applying. This usually comes in the form of a *diplôme* (diploma) that is awarded after a *concours* (competitive exam) at the end of a period of training. This worked well when there were jobs for almost all of those who managed to get their *diplôme*. But today's labour market is much more hostile, and it is impossible to guarantee that jobs will be available. This means that hundreds of thousands of people spend time and money working towards multiple *diplômes* without any guarantee they will be employed at the end of it.

Unemployment has not simply distorted the French economy. It has also become tied up with acute social problems. Perhaps the most visible of these has been the deterioration of post-war housing projects across the country. Tower blocks in the so-called *grands ensembles* (large estates) that were supposed to mark the advent of a fairer, more modern society began to fall into a state of disrepair from the late 1970s onwards, partly as a result of the use of substandard building materials. Amidst the worsening conditions, families who had enough disposable income moved away and were replaced by those further down the economic ladder, many of whom were immigrants. These people – and their children – found themselves stranded when the economic crisis deepened in the 1980s. Unemployment rates in these neighbourhoods quickly soared to 20% or 30%, far higher amongst young people. In some places, more than half of the active population were out of work, with little to do except loiter or engage in petty crime. Unlike the slumdwellers of the *bidonvilles*, for whom each day was a struggle for survival, the inhabitants of the *grands ensembles* were living in a dream that had turned rotten. The promise of urban renewal – one of the great symbols of post-war modernization – had given way to deprivation and social exclusion.

This situation came to a head in the 1990s and 2000s. By this time, the grandiose term *grand ensemble* had been replaced in the public imagination by the word *banlieue* (suburb). The increasingly sinister imaginary behind this term was vividly captured in Mathieu Kassovitz's epoch-making film *La Haine*

(1995), which told the story of three young *banlieue* residents as they tried to find a place for themselves in French society. Kassovitz's depiction was sensitive and empathetic, but for most French people at the time, the *banlieues* were the unruly, violent and overwhelmingly non-white counterpart to the picture-postcard France of vineyards and *châteaux*. In the same year that *La Haine* was released, Jacques Chirac fought his successful presidential campaign on the theme of insecurity and the *fracture sociale* (social fracture). The fear of the *banlieues* was a prominent part of this rhetoric. Chirac promised he would reunite France and heal the wounds caused by years of economic stagnation. But this is not what happened. Ten years later in 2005 – and with Chirac still in power – the country went up in flames in some of the worst urban unrest in the twentieth century. The immediate catalyst was the death of two teenagers who had taken refuge in an electrical substation in an attempt to flee a police spot-check in Clichy-sous-Bois in northeastern Paris. Over the next two weeks, residents of *banlieues* across France responded with violent attacks on the police and systematic destruction of property. In total, almost 10,000 cars were burned, and 3,000 people were arrested. As much as anything, the inchoate rage of many of the rioters was a cry for help – a desperate plea for recognition and investment after decades of discrimination and neglect.

Some sort of status quo has been restored since 2005, but few of the underlying problems have been resolved. Unemployment rates in depressed neigh-bourhoods remain extremely high, and police violence is endemic. In some places, trust between residents and public authorities is irreparably damaged. While many middle-class French people continue to bene-fit from the infrastructure, legislation and protections that were put in place during the post-war economic boom, those who live in the *banlieues* have been sys-tematically excluded from these gains. Many of them are the children of migrants who were brought to work in France during the boom only to be told in the late 1970s that they were no longer welcome. Today, they experience the sharp end of spatial, class and racial discrimination. They live far from city centres, forced to take overcrowded public transport to go to work; they are clearly identifiable by their accent and slang; and they find themselves looked over in favour of job applicants who are whiter and live in more palatable neighbourhoods. In the same way that the protests of 1968 threw into sharp relief the persistence of certain hierarchies in French society, the riots of 2005 were a reminder of France's inability to distribute equally the wealth and social protections of which it was so proud during the boom years.

France's ongoing social crisis has not remained entirely inaudible, though. It has permeated public discourse in the form of an acute collective crisis of confidence. This is reflected in large-scale polls and surveys since the 2000s, which confirm that the French are the most 'depressed' people in Europe, with the most 'pessimistic' outlook towards the future. Each year, dozens of popular books and essays come out about how the French have become 'schizophrenic', 'ill' and 'anxious' about the present. This sense of decadence has been compounded by the enthusiasm with which the French have embraced the xenophobic nationalism of the extreme right, and the visible decline of French influence overseas. Far from being the open and confident country of Gaullist myth, twenty-first-century France has increasingly appeared to itself and others as an insular and divided nation. Although many commentators continue to point out that social conditions and inequalities in France are not nearly as bad as perceptions would suggest – and that the standard of living is high compared to other developed countries – there is a lingering sense that France could be so much more than it is. Such a belief is not entirely irrational; it rests on memories of the post-war boom. If the French feel today that their country is in decline, it is because they are still struggling to escape from the shadow of Gaullist grandeur.

# 4

# Left and Right

Everyone with a working knowledge of politics recognizes the words 'left' and 'right'. But not everyone knows that these concepts originated in France. It was on 28 August 1789, at the height of the first phase of the French Revolution, that people first used these words to describe political groupings. On that day, the recently formed parliament – the Assemblée nationale constituante – was called upon to vote on the future role of the king. Those seated on the right wanted him to play a key part in government, along the lines of Britain's constitutional monarchy; those on the left only wanted to give him temporary veto power over any legislation passed by parliament. In the final vote, the advocates of the latter – the 'left' – won by a majority of 673 to 325.

Quite apart from inaugurating a new, more radical phase of the Revolution, this vote durably fixed the geography of political affiliation. Henceforth, the supporters of 'progress' sat on the left and the partisans of 'reaction' sat on the right. Even if the revolutionaries themselves did not have a clear or stable idea about who belonged on either side – and politicians routinely switched between them – the broad contours of this split quickly became embedded in French politics. Throughout the nineteenth century, those on the left fought to fulfil the egalitarian promise of the French Revolution through an increasingly radical set of political changes, while those on the right did what they could to slow down or stop this progress. So strong was the dichotomy between left and right that even political movements that had not existed in 1789 – like socialism, communism and fascism – were forced to identify themselves with one or other side of the divide.

## The French Left: The Children of the Revolution

Of the two camps, the left has always had the stronger, more cohesive identity. This is largely because those on the left have been identified with – and have identified themselves as – the rightful heirs to the radical ideals of the French Revolution. During the Revolution itself, it was the left that pushed for the abolition of the monarchy in 1792, and it was the same people who led the post-revolutionary struggle to remove Charles X, which culminated in the July Revolution of 1830. Subsequently, it was the left that kept alive the flame of republicanism and parliamentary government during the dark years of authoritarian rule by Napoleon III from 1851 to 1870. And, under the Third Republic, it was the left that saw off the final threat of the restoration of the monarchy by defeating the various royalist factions in the late 1870s. Even as the shadow of the Revolution faded in the latter decades of the twentieth century, the left remained at the forefront of opposition to any form of autocratic rule – from de Gaulle's democratic dictatorship in the 1960s to Macron's muscular presidentialism in the late 2010s.

The French left's strong identity was reinforced in the second half of the nineteenth century by the emergence of socialism. This political movement already had followers in France in the 1830s, but it crystallized in the late 1840s around the writings of Marx and Engels. Like all those on the left, socialists were concerned to defend and extend the legacy of the French Revolution, but their commitment to strongly egalitarian principles, anticlericalism, economic redistribution, the socialization of goods and the emancipation of working people gave them a more radical edge. As a result, they spent much of their time exhorting the left to be more left-wing. It was largely due to pressure from – or a fear of – socialism that improved labour laws and basic social security systems were implemented in the late nineteenth century, and Church and State were formally separated in 1905.

The Bolshevik Revolution of 1917 was a significant milestone not just for the French left, but for the left everywhere. For the first time, a major European state was governed according to explicitly socialist principles. The French state – like every other European state – now had to take seriously the threat of socialist revolution. This vastly increased the power of French socialists, who could demand wide-reaching social change with Bolshevism as their ally. But 1917 was a double-edged sword. While it proved that socialism was a viable governing ideology, it precipitated a catastrophic political split, as the left began to quarrel over the value and importance of the Bolshevik model. This culminated in the schism of the early 1920s when thousands of European socialists, angry at the perceived gradualism of the socialist movement, decided to create communist parties that would embody the Bolshevik ideology of revolution and social transformation. In France, this split took place at the congress of the Section française de l'internationale ouvrière (SFIO) in Tours in December 1920. After five days of acrimonious discussion, a majority of delegates voted for the creation of a new party, which soon became known as the Parti communiste français (PCF).

Although both socialists and communists belonged to the left after 1920, they regarded each other with, at best, suspicion and, at worst, outright contempt. For much of the 1920s, this tension was exacerbated by the 'class-against-class' strategy that was dictated to European communist parties by Moscow. This stipulated that the reformism of most socialist movements was counter-revolutionary and needed to be combated as fiercely as any opponents on the right. In response, communists everywhere adopted aggressive tactics towards their socialist counterparts and denounced their former comrades as 'reactionaries'. The rise of fascism led to a belated change of strategy in the mid-1930s, as the Soviets urged communists everywhere to forge alliances to block the radical right. This led to the creation of the ill-fated, but hugely symbolic, Popular Front governments in France and Spain, which were made up of a coalition of left-wing parties. But it was too little, too late: the Popular Front government in France collapsed after less than two years, and its Spanish cousin was defeated by Franco's Nationalist armies in the Spanish Civil War. Worse still, as Europe rushed headlong into the Second World War, communists and socialists together found themselves brutally swept away by the armies of Hitler and Mussolini, often with the help of other compliant governments (including that of Vichy France).

But the persecution of socialists and communists during the war did not lead to their disappearance. On the contrary, the left came back stronger in 1945, partly due to its association with resistance movements in Europe, and partly due to the enormous prestige of the Soviet Union after its victory over Nazism. In France, this manifested itself in the spectacular electoral success of the PCF, which secured 25% or more of the vote in every legislative election from 1945 to 1956. This vote share began to decline in the late 1950s and 1960s, but the PCF still managed to gain more than 20% of the vote in most legislative elections until the end of the 1970s. In addition, it wielded substantial power at a local level, especially in its fiefdoms in northern and eastern Paris – the so-called *ceinture*

*rouge* (red belt) – and industrial areas in the north near
Lille and in the south near Marseille. With a devoted
membership of several hundred thousand, strong
links to the CGT trade union and voter numbers of 5
million or more, the PCF was a vital part of the culture
of the left in France until the 1980s. Thanks to rigor-
ous party discipline, it also kept the same name and
structure for the entire post-war period. Young communists who go out campaigning today are the only
activists in France who belong to the same political
movement as their predecessors in 1945.

The socialists in post-war France were not as organized or disciplined as the PCF, but they had more
influence in national government. Most of them were
still grouped in – and fought elections as – the SFIO
or in one of the small 'radical-socialist' or progressive
parties. The SFIO did not command the same vote
share as the PCF, but still averaged around 15–20%
in legislative elections until the early 1960s. Crucially,
the SFIO was a partner in almost every government
in this period. More palatable to their moderate parliamentary brethren, and more willing to enter into
power-sharing agreements with centrist groups,
socialists helped to prop up the ever-changing roster
of government coalitions that were a defining feature
of the Fourth Republic. Some of the most prominent
political personalities of the 1950s – including Guy
Mollet and Pierre Mendès-France – were socialists,
and they exerted a substantial influence over the formation of post-war social and economic policy.

In the 1960s, the power of the SFIO and its allies began to wane. There were three main reasons for this. First was their complicity in France's colonial wars. Mollet, in particular, is remembered as the leader who accorded 'special powers' to the French military in Algeria in 1956, a decision that led to state-sponsored violence by the army on an unprecedented scale. These actions, along with a long-standing benevolent attitude to French imperialism, enraged many left-wing anti-colonial activists, who deserted the party in droves. Second, the electoral system de Gaulle created for the Fifth Republic – and, above all, the institution of the directly elected president – meant no party of the left could aspire to executive power since they could not command a sufficient vote share. This was not so important for communists, whose political identity revolved around a hostile attitude to the workings of the 'bourgeois' state, but the inability to compete at a national level was terminal for the SFIO. Finally, the protests of 1968 showed that the most dynamic movements within the non-communist left were no longer located in the SFIO. Instead, young left-wing activists were increasingly turning to radical social movements more suited to the insurgent politics of the late 1960s.

The decline of the SFIO was, in some ways, a blessing for the French left because it opened the possibility of renewal. This duly came in the early 1970s with the creation of the new Parti socialiste (PS) under the leadership of the mercurial François Mitterrand.

Mitterrand – who had been in politics since the 1940s
– was not a natural man of the left. He had no history
as a left-wing activist and only the scantiest knowledge of Marxism. But perhaps because he was not
embroiled in the culture of the French left, he saw
clearly the main obstacle ahead. He understood that,
unless the French left was united, it would never
gain power under the Fifth Republic. With this aim
in mind, he single-mindedly set about eliminating or
co-opting his opponents. Within the PS, he ruthlessly
outflanked the leaders of alternative 'tendencies' and,
outside the PS, he negotiated a common platform
with the PCF to ensure their electoral cooperation.
This strategy soon bore fruit. The united left came
within a whisker of securing a parliamentary majority in 1978 and triumphed in 1981, when Mitterrand
won the presidency and the left won a huge majority.
Together, the PS, PCF and its allies gained 333 out of
491 seats, the highest proportion of seats ever for the
left in modern French history.

Mitterrand remained president until 1995, winning
a second term in 1988. His party, however, did not
fare so well. There was great hope attached to the new
government in 1981, and it implemented major social
reforms. But the economic climate was unpropitious
for state- and demand-led macroeconomic policies.
After two years of enormous spending and several
emergency devaluations of the currency, Mitterrand
declared an 'about-turn' in 1983 and announced the
need for austerity measures to stabilize the economy.

In a depressed economic climate, which was made worse by mushrooming unemployment, the PS struggled to maintain its support base and was defeated in the legislative elections of 1986. It returned to power in 1988, along with Mitterrand, but was again defeated in 1993. It was increasingly clear that the PS was finding it difficult to adapt to a changing working-class electorate, which was more and more tempted by the extreme right. After 1995, there were moments of light – a parliamentary majority from 1997 to 2002 and the presidency of François Hollande from 2007 to 2012 – but the downward trend was unmistakable. In the election of 2017, the PS was almost completely obliterated from the electoral map: its presidential candidate, Benoît Hamon, scored a dismal 6.4%; the party was reduced to a mere 30 *députés* in the Assemblée nationale; and a wave of PS municipalities changed hands, thereby destroying one of the great strengths of the party, its local power base.

The PCF would have taken some satisfaction in the precipitous decline of the PS were it not for the fact that it, too, fell apart in this period. Already in the 1980s, Mitterrand's PS had begun to siphon votes away from the PCF and, by the 1990s, the party had been terminally damaged by the collapse of communism in the Soviet Union. In the 2000s, its support base dwindled, and even its local fiefdoms started to change hands. The PCF still exists today, but it rarely fights elections alone. More often than not, it is part of a broader conglomerate of far-left movements or 'left front'. This grouping is currently known as La France insoumise (LFI, Unbowed France) and is led by the ex-PS politician Jean-Luc Mélenchon. The LFI has become a home for many ex-communists and disillusioned socialists, and it has achieved some modest electoral gains, not least in the 2017 presidential election, when Mélenchon scored almost 20% of the vote in the first round. Nevertheless, it is hard to avoid the feeling that the entire organized French left – from moderate socialist to hard-bitten communist – has been in a process of managed decline since the turn of the century.

It would be a mistake, though, to reduce the post-war French left merely to its successes and failures at the ballot box. Since the nineteenth century, the culture of the left in France has depended at least as much on grassroots mobilization as it has on electoral legitimacy. Hence, for much of the twentieth century, French communists focused as much of their energy on bringing working people together in trade unions, protests and social gatherings as they did in contesting elections. Communist municipalities had community centres and self-help groups that anchored factories, neighbourhoods and entire communities. Through commemoration and mythification, communist activists memorialized the Paris Commune of 1871, the Popular Front and the Communist Resistance, weaving these together to create a multi-generational memory of struggle, loss and triumph. Of course, many PCF members had to grapple with the crimes of the Soviet Union, but this often came second to the deep feeling of belonging to a genuine political family.

French socialism had a no less elevated pedigree, going back to some of the great leaders of the Third Republic like Jean Jaurès, as well as the Popular Front. Moreover, Socialists could proudly proclaim that they were not tainted by the horrors of Bolshevism, especially after the suppression of the Hungarian Revolution in 1956 and the revelations of Stalin's crimes at the Twentieth Congress of the Communist Party of the Soviet Union in the same year. More recently, socialists rightly maintain that, since the 1970s, they have been at the forefront of some of the most interesting experiments in municipal governance in post-war France and that they have spurred on the growth of a vast array of civil society organizations. At the height of its power in the 1980s and 1990s, the PS supported a huge web of cultural, artistic and educational initiatives that collectively transformed the shape of French society. These were not explicitly political in the same way as the PCF's community centres and trade unions, but they contributed to a flourishing of a grassroots left-wing culture, the legacies of which are still visible today in cultural policy, the urban landscape and the representation of minority communities.

Lastly, we should acknowledge the many other left-wing personalities and movements that have existed at various points in post-war France. The list of these is almost endless, but some highlights include the anti-colonial activists in the 1950s who campaigned tirelessly against the crimes committed by the French across the imperial world; the student unions that thrived in the rapidly expanding higher education sector from the 1960s onwards; radical artists – like the Situationists in the 1960s – who have given to the French left some of its most memorable imagery; Arlette Laguiller, the leader of the Trotskyist party Lutte Ouvrière, who stood again and again in every presidential election from 1973 to 2007 without ever gaining more than 5% of the vote; and the constellation of anti-capitalist and anti-globalization movements that periodically take to the streets to protest against the inequities of twenty-first-century capitalism.

Individually, these movements and personalities have rarely troubled the authorities in power, nor have they been very good at cooperating in the service of a defined political cause. But, at certain moments, they have found themselves at the heart of political debate. This was the case, for instance, with anti-colonial activists at the tail end of the Algerian War or the Situationists in 1968. These brief moments in the limelight have usually been enough to keep the flame alive. Most people on the left in France are accustomed to failure – so much so that some political scientists argue that the expectation of failure is a key reason why the French left has struggled to remain in government for extended periods of time – but the most dedicated activists never cease to believe that change is possible. They know that their ideas cannot command a majority, but this is less important than exposing the inequalities of the present and the hypocrisy of their right-wing opponents. It is not difficult to find flaws in the political and economic configuration of France in the twenty-first century, and left-wing activists are uniquely placed to highlight them. After all, this is exactly what they have been doing since 1789.

Inevitably, such an acute awareness of contemporary socio-economic problems has meant that both the radical extra-parliamentary left and the moderate left have a strong tradition of direct action. Amongst other things, this has fuelled France's reputation as a land of strikes and protests, even though it has the lowest rate of unionization in Europe (only 8.8% in 2018, compared to 16.5% in Germany, 23.4% in the United Kingdom and 65% in Sweden). Not a month goes by without a demonstration against a proposed law or a strike by a major trade union. Students routinely barricade the entrances to their school buildings and lecture halls, while workers walk out of their places of employment in wildcat or planned strike action. Every year truckers blockade petrol refineries, farmers burn fruit on the motorway and disgruntled protesters occupy town squares and roads. Not all these protests are in the name of the left, but the overwhelming majority claim some association with a left-wing party or movement. This, too, is part of the left's revolutionary heritage. Generations of left-wing activists have played out their revolutionary dreams on the street and the factory floor and, in many cases, they have succeeded in rolling back reforms or extracting additional benefits from employers.

The French left, then, has punched above its electoral weight. Apart from a few moments when it has been able to unite behind a common programme, it has rarely had a majority in the Assemblée nationale, but its influence has stretched far and wide across metropolitan France and beyond. Today, when its electoral base seems weaker than ever, it is this tapestry of connections, imaginations and mobilizations that holds it together. When the time comes for the left to re-emerge, it will need to rely on all of these to forge a new coalition of people who still believe in fighting for the promise of progress. This is not a foregone conclusion: as many have argued, the French revolutionary tradition all but expired in the 1990s. Since then, the French left has struggled to identify a workable platform for its ideas. For it to survive, it will have to reckon without the historical reference point that underpinned its identity for more than two centuries. Still, if there is one thing for which the left is famous, it is triumph in adversity. When the revolution returns, it may not look much like 1789, but it will almost certainly see the left play a starring role.

### The French Right: From Counter-Revolution to Technocracy (and Back)

Where the history of the French left is saturated with shattered utopias, moments of revolutionary hope and dramatic betrayals, the history of the French right appears either banal or illegible, especially after 1945. At first glance, there seems to be little to distinguish the succession of competing centre-right parties – all with different acronyms – and it is often difficult to identify which middle-aged man in a suit is in charge at any given moment. Some people do stand out – de Gaulle, obviously, and personalities like Pierre Poujade and Jean-Marie Le Pen – but many influential figures of the post-war right like Jean Lecanuet, Antoine Pinay, Jean-Pierre Raffarin or Raymond Barre have receded into the pages of history books. They – and their ideas – survive only in the memories of those who worked with them or follow in their footsteps.

There are many reasons for this amnesia about the history of the right. One of the most important is the lack of a coherent doctrine or ideology. As many have pointed out, it is easier to say what the French right is against than what it is for. Unlike communists or socialists, who have revelled in their mythical past, the right has struggled to find a common set of stories on which it can rely. This has made it correspondingly difficult for historians – and even the general public – to say exactly what the French right is about. But the problem may be one of interpretation, rather than fact. The idea that a political party or movement is more legitimate when it has a clearly defined ideological platform is a by-product of the history of the left. If we think instead of politics in terms of moods, emotions or reflexes, the history of the French right becomes easier to decipher. Seen this way, the French right has been, in its moderate form, a standard-bearer of stability over revolution, and, in its radical form, a passionate opponent of the gospel of progress. If nothing else, the right has been defined by its struggle with the left over the meaning of some of the most important political symbols in France – from the 'nation' to the 'people'. This binary collision has shaped modern French politics and looks likely to do so for some time to come.

The oppositional character of the right has its origins in the political turmoil of the French Revolution. From 1789 onwards, those on the right focused their energies on containing the progressive ideas that had been unleashed by the Revolution. When in power, the right tried to arrest or reverse the gains of the Revolution by criticizing its assumptions and outcomes. As was the case on the left, the right was not unified in its approach. Moderate conservatives and liberals accepted the realities of the new revolutionary order but hoped to maintain aspects of hierarchy and tradition, whereas the radical right denounced the Revolution and looked for ways to bring back the monarchy, the Catholic Church, the pre-revolutionary *ancien régime* or all three of these things at once. Still, there was an understanding that the main purpose of the right was to oppose any manifestations of 'progress', often by appealing to deep-seated fears of social disorder, or by conjuring up images of religious apocalypse.

Over the course of the nineteenth century, the French right gradually coalesced around three strands: a 'legitimist' strand, which was radically counter-revolutionary and monarchist; an 'Orleanist' strand, which defended constitutional monarchy and liberal economic principles; and a 'Bonapartist' strand, which emphasized the primacy of the all-powerful individual sovereign. These three strands gave shape to the parliamentary and extra-parliamentary right all the way through to the Second World War. The legitimist strand encompassed a whole variety of radical groups, from ultramontane Catholic organizations to the well-known nationalist, xenophobic and proto-fascist movement Action française. The Orleanist strand was taken up by many of the leading architects of the Third Republic, who tried to temper the reforming zeal of those on the left, while still accepting the necessity of republican government. Finally, the 'Bonapartist' strand was embodied by Napoleon III in the 1850s and 1860s but returned to haunt France in the form of the Vichy government, which was entirely built around the legend of Pétain.

These three strands were clearly visible in the fractious politics of the 1920s and 1930s, during which the French right commanded substantial intellectual and political influence. But this influence began to unravel after 1940 as defeat and occupation undermined the Vichy regime's attempts to implement a properly right-wing 'National Revolution'. By the end of the war, the right was in poor shape. The left was marching forwards at the ballot box, the extreme right had been roundly defeated and the centre-right was tainted by its association with the downfall of the Third Republic. Some right-wing ideas disappeared altogether after the war: royalism, for instance, largely evaporated since no one seriously believed in the restoration of the monarchy. More moderate strands of the right, such as Christian democracy, did survive the war, and they played an active role in many of the governing coalitions of the Fourth Republic. They were also central to the construction of European institutions, especially in the form of Robert Schuman, who is often considered to be one of the founding fathers of the European project. But it was not until the 1960s – and the presidency of de Gaulle – that the French right truly made a comeback.

Although de Gaulle himself had a complicated relationship with political labels, usually preferring to regard himself as above the party-political fray, he did more than any other politician to reactivate the Bonapartist strand of the French right during his eleven-year presidency. He was careful never to undermine the rule of law, but his contempt for parliament and his centralization of executive power came very close to a form of democratic authoritarianism. This long-lasting and successful adaptation of right-wing political values to a post-war context almost single-handedly reshaped the French right. After his death, right-wing politicians immediately started to invoke the spirit of de Gaulle, and the major party of the centre-right proudly proclaimed that it was 'Gaullist' in its orientation. Half a century later, most of the French right remains enthusiastic about de Gaulle's achievement in uniting the right in the service of a project of national renewal.

The revival of the centre-right in the 1960s was followed by the return of the extreme right in the 1980s. The main vehicle for this was the Front National (FN), which was created in 1973 by amalgamating a disparate collection of extreme right groups associated with royalism, racism and the defence of French colonialism. For its first decade, it made relatively little progress, but, from the early 1980s onwards, it began to make its presence felt at the ballot box, in part by shedding some of its more arcane ideas and embracing populist, nationalist and anti-immigrant themes. This period of growth culminated in the 2002 presidential election, when the FN's colourful leader, Jean-Marie Le Pen, shocked the country by reaching the second round at the expense of the PS candidate, Lionel Jospin. This was a reminder that, after many decades of quiescence, the embers of the counter-revolutionary right were still burning. At a time when the French revolutionary tradition seemed to be on its way out, the growing presence of the FN suggested that the extreme right had somehow found a way to survive in changing times.

The success of the FN in the 1990s and 2000s led to a belated upsurge of scholarly interest in right-wing politics, as researchers scrambled to understand a tradition they believed had disappeared. After decades of stagnant scholarship, dozens of books and articles began to be published every year about the dangers of the 'new' extreme right – a trend that continues today. But it is somewhat paradoxical that it should have taken the rise of an extreme right party to draw attention to the transformations of the post-war French right. Despite France's reputation as a land of left-wing revolution, the electoral statistics show that it has long been dominated by the right. In the six or so decades since the inauguration of the Fifth Republic in 1958, there has been a left-wing majority in parliament for only 20 years and a left-wing president for 19. The rest of the time, the country has been governed by different strands of the right, from de Gaulle's grand alliance and Nicolas Sarkozy's conservative bloc, to Valéry Giscard d'Estaing's and Emmanuel Macron's liberal-centrist parties. If there is any such thing as a national political orientation in contemporary France, it points decidedly to the right.

There are several explanations for this. At a very general level, the success of the right in post-war France is a consequence of a deep fear of disorder, unrest and revolution. It is no coincidence that the largest ever majority for the right in the Assemblée nationale came immediately after the protests of 1968. To many French people, it looked as if the country was on the verge of political collapse. A vote for the right was a vote for stability. Similar processes were at work in 1995 and 2007, when Chirac and Sarkozy won the presidential elections. On both occasions, the electoral cycle was dominated by discussions of recent or ongoing riots and strikes. By electing right-wing parties and leaders in these years, the French wanted to limit the potential for further instability.

This fear of disorder has been reinforced by the lingering presence of Catholicism. As most historians of French politics know, religious observance was – until the 1970s – one of the most reliable indicators of political affiliation. The more Catholic the person, the town or the region, the more likely they were to vote for the right. This meant that the strongly Catholic Atlantic coast was staunchly right-wing, while south and southwestern France, where religious obser- vance was lower, leaned to the left. These rigid pat- terns gradually began to come apart from the 1970s onwards as people abandoned the Catholic Church in large numbers, but they remain important. Even if much explicitly Catholic language has disappeared from politics in the twenty-first century, debates around issues such as national identity, reproductive rights and Islam quickly bring forth Catholic moral and political tropes. In particular, the French right has benefited from the outrage that has accompanied the proliferation of Islamic dress and prayer rituals, as well as legislation to legalize gay marriage and open assisted reproduction technologies to same-sex couples. As the left has positioned itself as the cham- pion of socially permissive policies, the right has been able to present itself as the defender of traditional 'French' values.

Beyond these broad explanations for the long-term success of the right, there are others that apply to specific strands and traditions. For instance, it is impossible to understand the liberal presidencies of Giscard d'Estaing and Macron – both of which echoed their nineteenth-century Orleanist predecessors – without recognizing the electoral power of a new class of educated, urban elites. These people were products of the post-war boom. They often considered themselves at the centre of the political spectrum and espoused liberal views on economics and society. In the absence of an explicitly 'liberal' party, they usually had to choose a candidate or party clearly to the left or to the right. But, in the mid-1970s and the mid-2010s, they had the opportunity to vote for someone who looked and sounded like them. Giscard d'Estaing and Macron were both gifted young technocrats who came to power promising liberal reforms and a break with France's stultifying administrative traditions. Significantly, both leaders tried to present themselves as neither right nor left. The problem was that, in a strongly bi-partisan system, the realities of power and the difficulties of implementing reforms meant finding partners amongst the traditional parties of the left and right – and, on both occasions, it was with the right that they most readily made common cause. In the case of Giscard d'Estaing, this made the later years of his presidency distinctly right-wing in their focus on immigration and the threat of a unified socialist and communist government; there are signs that Macron's presidency will end in the same way.

As for the extreme right, it has benefited from the socio-economic transformations that took place after the economic slowdown of the 1970s. Much of the electoral success of the FN – now rebaptized the Rassemblement National (RN, National Rally) – has been driven by shifting allegiances in working-class communities that abandoned the PCF in the deindustrializing wave of the 1980s. The extreme right stepped in to exploit this political vacuum. Except for the *ceinture rouge* around Paris, which remains a bastion of the left, the map of RN support today mirrors almost exactly the map of PCF support in the 1950s. The extreme right now governs various small and medium-sized towns in the north around Lille and Roubaix, and in the southern parts of the Rhône valley, near Avignon and Marseille. It has also made inroads into the Languedoc, Alsace and Lorraine, and rural areas around Orléans. In all these places, the RN's message – that France has too many immigrants and has too readily embraced the diktats of global capitalism – has found a sympathetic audience.

The extreme right continues to face substantial challenges. The RN and its current leader – Marine Le Pen – are primarily recipients of protest votes; most people do not consider them a credible party of government. In addition, many RN policies, especially those that relate to 'national preference' and the exclusion of foreigners from public services, are unconstitutional and unpopular. Above all, the RN has had very little experience of actual governance. It has almost no *députés* in the Assemblée nationale (8 out of 577 in 2017), and it has far fewer mayors and municipal councillors than any of the other major parties. This weakness has made the party acutely dependent on the presidential election, which is the only time it can compete directly in France's two-round voting system. Although Marine Le Pen, like her father, managed to progress to the second round in 2017, she found herself blocked by a severe credibility deficit. Her subsequent defeat sent the party into a downward spiral similar to, if not as serious as, the one that swept through the party after 2002.

Nevertheless, there is a case to be made that the rise of the extreme right represents the biggest recomposition of the French right since de Gaulle's presidency in the 1960s. The main Gaullist centre-right party, currently known as Les Républicains (LR), remains the natural home for a conservative right-wing electorate, but the rapid rise of Macron to the left and sustained pressure from the RN on the right are reshaping the political spectrum. If this shift were to be confirmed in the next decade, it would lead to a major crisis for the main parties of the right and the left. This is because the architecture of the Fifth Republic was built around the twin principles of bipolarity and stability. The two-round voting system was designed so that voters could choose from the full diversity of French political opinion in the first round but would then be limited to representatives of the main parties of the right and left in the second round. The idea was to stabilize a volatile parliamentary system by forcing voters to make a 'sensible' choice in the second round.

For the right, this system worked well from the start since they were largely united under de Gaulle and therefore easily able to form majority administrations. It took longer for the left to master the electoral game because the left-wing vote was divided between socialists and communists, but they finally did so under Mitterrand in the 1970s. This predictable bipolarity, in which the centre-right and centre-left alternated presidents and governments, was shaken in 2002. This was the first time a non-mainstream candidate reached the second round of the presidential election. The PS was able to recover enough in subsequent years to restore a semblance of bipolarity to the various legislative and presidential elections that took place in 2007 and 2012. But in 2017 the French again rejected the rules of the game, except this time no candidate from a mainstream party reached the second round of the presidential election at all. Instead, voters had to choose between Macron – a politician with no party affiliation and almost no experience of political office – and Marine Le Pen – who represented the extreme right. What was even more troubling was that relatively few people seemed to be concerned about this outcome. Indeed, polling and public opinion data suggest that the French are more ready than ever for a new political configuration.

Does this mean that the age-old division between left and right is coming apart? There are certainly signs that this is happening. With the legacy of the French Revolution no more than a distant memory, voters no longer strictly identify with left or right, nor do they have the same commitment to specific political parties. Some of the most pressing public debates over citizenship, European integration and globalization cross party lines in unexpected ways. And the growing importance of single-issue social movements focused on, say, the environment or gay rights has made the broad categories of left and right less attractive. Nevertheless, it is unlikely that the ideas of left and right will disappear entirely in the next few years. Not only is it difficult to erase 250 years of French political history, but it is not clear that the various attempts on the part of politicians like Macron and Marine Le Pen to craft a new political identity will succeed. There have been many attempts to transcend the political affiliations that crystallized during the French Revolution. In the late 1790s, Napoleon tried to put to rest the violent political divisions of the early revolutionary years by promising national unity and military triumph; de Gaulle did something similar in the 1950s when he urged the French to forget the divisive memories of occupation, decolonization and class conflict. But, in each case, the pull of bipolarity was too great. Within a few years, new lefts and

new rights emerged to reimpose a strong binary structure on the political landscape. It remains to be seen
whether, in the twenty-first century, the French can
really do without the ideas of left and right. If so, it
would mark a political revolution almost as profound
as the one that gave birth to these ideas in the first
place.

# 5

# The Republic and
# Its Discontents

At some point, most visitors to France will have encountered the official logo used by a whole range of state institutions. It features a profile portrait of Marianne, similar to the one on the front cover of this book, against a background of the blue, white and red of the French flag. Underneath this image are the words 'Liberté, Égalité, Fraternité' and, below this, 'République Française' in capital letters. Its use is so widespread that it feels as if it has existed for centuries, but in fact it was only created in 1999 by an advertising firm. Like many other things in France, the state's official logo is an invented tradition. It is a very recent symbol that is supposed to capture an age-old institution. But the marketing gurus who came up with the official logo did not create it out of nothing. They were working in a context of deep anxiety in the 1990s about French national identity and the meaning of citizenship. Their creation was supposed to be a response to this anxiety. They wanted to squeeze as many unifying symbols of the French nation into one image as possible: the tricolour flag, the bust of Marianne, the highly symbolic slogan of 'liberté, égalité, fraternité' and – most importantly – an unambiguous reference to France's identity as a republic.

The latter was no accident. More than any other language of politics, republicanism has become the dominant way in which the French talk about their country, their past and their society. In the twenty-first century, France is not just a republic in a formal, technical sense; it is – or at least tries to be – the embodiment of republican *values*. What exactly these are has been the subject of ardent debate over the years, but a fairly uncontroversial list might include: an opposition to monarchy and a suspicion of executive authority; the embrace of representative government; a robust conception of citizenship and civic participation; a commitment to rationality and the rule of law; some form of secularism, often wrapped up in a strongly anticlerical discourse; and an emphasis on the emancipatory power of the state. These values have provided a guiding thread for republicans from the late eighteenth century to the present day – and they have affected everything from the way the French state is organized to the way French people interact with each other.

### The Chequered History of French Republicanism

One of the common misconceptions about French republicanism is that it has been the governing philosophy of France since 1789. This is not true. The fact that France is now on its fifth republic should give an indication of how difficult it has been to construct a republican state. The First Republic, born in

September 1792 out of the abolition of the monarchy during the French Revolution, is the founding myth of French republicanism. It was during this time that the country began its long journey to becoming an egalitarian, rational parliamentary democracy. This dream, which many would argue is still unfulfilled today, was unceremoniously terminated by Napoleon in 1804 when he declared France an empire. This was followed by almost half a century of non-republican government, ranging from authoritarian military rule to constitutional monarchy. The Second Republic met a similar fate. Inaugurated during the February Revolution of 1848, it too was ended by the imposition of imperial rule in 1852, this time at the hands of Napoleon III, who governed France until 1870. During this period – known as the Second Empire – many passionate defenders of republican values were sent into exile, and the possibility of a truly republican government seemed a distant dream.

The Third Republic, which was proclaimed in September 1870, lasted longer than either of its predecessors, a full 70 years in total. It has since become associated with some of the greatest achievements of French republicanism, including the universal provision of education, the expansion of the French language, the construction of thousands of civic buildings and monuments, and the formal separation of Church and State in 1905. It was also the Third Republic that successfully galvanized the French into defending their country during the First World

War. The result was a political system that was strong enough to withstand the authoritarian wave of the 1920s and 1930s. Nevertheless, as we saw earlier, each one of the Third Republic's achievements was met with bitter opposition from radical Catholics, disgruntled conservatives, rabid anti-Semites, revolutionary communists and many others. By the time the Third Republic collapsed in 1940, its legitimacy had frayed, and it had few supporters. Republicanism, it seemed, had served its time.

As with so many other things, the Second World War turned the status quo upside-down. Defeat and occupation made the restoration of legitimate state institutions an urgent imperative for the post-war elites. One of the few governing ideologies that could be salvaged from the crisis of the late 1930s was republicanism, and it was used as the basis of the constitution of the Fourth Republic. In its early years, this new regime commanded widespread support, but it was still vulnerable to attacks from the political extremes. To many, it looked as if the greatest threat would come from a powerful communist movement that continued to view republican democracy with suspicion. But, as we already know, it was the ghost of the extreme right that ultimately killed the Fourth Republic in the form of radical *pied-noir* groups who openly challenged the state in order to defend French Algeria. It took the return of de Gaulle to see off the extreme right, but even he was not willing to conform to the rules. By changing the constitution and inaugurating the Fifth

Republic in 1958, he again modified the meaning and substance of French republicanism.

As many people noted at the time, de Gaulle himself did not seem to embody traditional republican values. Although he ruled out any form of dictatorship, he was contemptuous of parliamentary sovereignty, preferred to talk about 'unity' rather than 'equality' and referred sparingly to the French Revolution. But his commitment to an idiosyncratic form of French republicanism did have one very important long-term consequence: it reconciled the French right to the Republic. This was a major historical shift. Since 1789, it was the left that had most enthusiastically embraced the language and ideas of republicanism. De Gaulle ensured that henceforth almost every political party would seek to identify itself with the French Republic, save for a few radical fringe movements of the left and right. This neutralized a long-standing desire on the right to dispense with the institutions of republican government and replace them with something more elitist or authoritarian. The clearest sign of de Gaulle's successful 'republicanization' of the right was that, by the 1970s, most political commentators believed that France had become a mature republic, broadly united around a common set of political values.

It was something of a surprise, then, to see the country's political elites once again squabbling over republican values barely 20 years later. To many people, the return of republicanism as a topic of political polemic seemed to be little more than a superficial rhetorical battle designed to conceal the absence of any real ideas in French politics. But it turned out to be rather more than that. In fact, the republicanism of the 1990s was a way of revitalizing politics after the ideological reorientations of the 1970s and 1980s. The explosion of a Marxist consensus in French intellectual life after the protests of 1968 and the atrophy of Gaullist ideas after de Gaulle's death had left an ideological void at the centre of French politics. In this context of ideological fragmentation, a growing number of historians, intellectuals and political actors began to turn to republicanism as a model of political action and community that could replace the lost ideals of Gaullist grandeur and revolutionary communism.

Initially, this 'neo-republican turn' was most clearly visible amongst the moderate socialist left. As François Mitterrand's socialist experiment ground to a halt in 1983 – and as the PS faced an unexpected challenge from the extreme right – young socialists began to lean more and more heavily on a form of progressive republicanism to boost their governing credentials. The collapse of the Berlin Wall, the bicentenary of the French Revolution and the first public controversy over the wearing of the Islamic headscarf – all of which took place in 1989 – hastened the conversion process. For many on the moderate left, republicanism was an attractive, ready-made alternative to an increasingly problematic socialist ideology, and it provided a way for disaffected socialists to rally to strong political values. It was also supported by intellectual fellow travellers of the left, like the publisher and historian Pierre Nora, or philosophers like Alain Finkielkraut and Régis Debray, all of whom effected transitions from youthful Marxism to middle-aged republicanism.

What was less clear at the time was the extent to which the right, too, had begun to domesticate this new form of republicanism. After a period in the 1980s when the centre right flirted with neo-liberal ideas of free markets and privatization, the 1990s saw a renewed emphasis on statism and national sovereignty, combined with a growing interest in republicanism. For instance, Jacques Chirac's invocation of the *fracture sociale* during his 1995 presidential election campaign drew on classic republican themes such as the fear of national disunity and the need for social integration – and he continued to use this language after his victory. The threat of Algerian terrorism in the 1990s and the growing visibility of Muslims in French society provided another point of entry for the right, which was able to deploy republican ideas in an effort to counter the alleged 'Islamization' of France. This was particularly noticeable in discussions surrounding *laïcité* (secularism). Once a value firmly associated with the crusading anticlericalism of the French left, by the early 2000s *laïcité* had become a rhetorical tool with which the right could denounce all public expressions of the Muslim faith, from the building of mosques to the wearing of the 'burqa'. It is hardly a coincidence that the 2004 law banning religious symbols in public schools and the 2010 ban on the covering of the face in public spaces should have coincided with periods of right-wing rule.

Even more surprising than the right's newfound passion for republicanism was the penetration of republican language on the extreme right. This began in earnest with the elevation of Marine Le Pen to the leadership of the FN in 2010. After more than two centuries during which the extreme right had poured scorn on republican language and symbolism, suddenly Le Pen's speeches were admonishing the French state for failing to uphold France's republican values and urging it to use a more pro-active *laïcité* to combat everything from Islamic terrorism to the distribution of halal meat. The irony of this strategy was not lost on horrified socialist politicians who realized the republicanism they had championed in the 1980s to combat the rise of the FN was now being used by the FN to attack them. To a degree, Le Pen's accommodation to neo-republicanism has served her well and her party has progressed in national, regional and European elections. But the French electorate have not been entirely fooled; they recognize the difference between the republicanism of the left and of the extreme right.

Still, the widespread use of republican language, ideas and symbols by centre-right and extreme right politicians is more than just a cheap electoral strategy. It suggests a further reinvention of republicanism. Where the republicanism that emerged in the

1970s and 1980s was dominated by themes dear to the French left – such as anticlerical secularism, revolutionary passion and the French school – it is quite possible that the republicanism of the 2010s and 2020s will be defined by themes that sit more comfortably with the right – such as anti-Muslim secularism, security and the morality of the public space. One sign of this shift was the public controversy in 2016 over the so-called 'burkini bans', which made it illegal to wear full-body bathing suits on the beach. These bans were enacted by a cluster of centre-right and extreme right mayors on the Côte d'Azur, who justified them as a form of republican *laïcité* that would preserve 'public order', 'security' and 'morality'. Even though the burkini bans were immediately abrogated by an appeal to France's highest legal authority, the Conseil d'État, they showed how a form of right-wing republicanism could develop in a region like southeastern France, which has long been a bastion of right-wing politics.

Given the frequent invocations of republican values by almost everyone in French politics, it is tempting to see these as little more than an empty vessel, ripe for manipulation. This would be a mistake. The resurgence of republicanism in political and intellectual life has gone hand-in-hand with a much larger civic debate about the way French society should be organized and the way it should manage diversity. Since the 1980s, France has faced unprecedented economic challenges in the form of slow growth, deindustrialization and unemployment. It has also had to contend with increasingly muscular forms of postcolonial identity politics and the decline of several key social institutions (notably trade unions and the Catholic Church). Lastly, the French state has embarked on ambitious plans to decentralize government administration within and beyond metropolitan France, as well as integrate French political and legal structures with those of the European Union. Taken together, these changes have left many people asking what it means to be French at all. In this context, republicanism has provided a plausible – if contradictory – answer.

For example, republican ideas have been widely invoked in discussions surrounding the negative consequences of economic change. In the face of long-term unemployment and poor working conditions, individuals and organizations have called on the country's *esprit républicain* (republican spirit) to heal the social divide. In so doing, they have been channelling ideas of fraternity and national union that have deep roots in the history of French republicanism. Republicanism has also penetrated debates about the future of the welfare state, with many people arguing that a defence of the welfare state must simultaneously involve a defence of France's 'unique' form of republicanism. The problem is that it is hard to connect republican values and economic policy in a consistent way. French republicanism is, first and foremost, about politics – that is, the institutions and values of government. Historically, defenders of republicanism have had very little to say about economic organization, and so it is difficult today to articulate republican values as a response to neo-liberal capitalism.

The French are on altogether firmer ground when they use republican symbols and languages against manifestations of identity politics. Indeed, the very public disagreements over the place of 'minorities' and 'communities' within French society have become one of the defining political debates of recent decades. On one side are those who argue that the existence of minority communities – especially religious and ethnic minority communities – is a normal part of the democratic process. On the other are those who maintain that the French republican tradition is resolutely opposed to specific communities that might pose a threat to national unity. To outsiders, this second line of reasoning often appears bizarre or intolerant, but it is anchored in modern French history. During the French Revolution, many revolutionaries worried that intermediary bodies between the citizen and the state – such as political parties or religious authorities – were a danger to the new republic. They feared that such bodies would dilute citizens' relationship with the state and lead to split allegiances. At a time when the Catholic Church was an existential threat to the Revolution, such concerns made sense.

More than two centuries later, few people doubt the authority and legitimacy of the republican state, but the anxiety about intermediary bodies persists. In particular, the recent upsurge in postcolonial identity politics has reopened questions about the potential danger of political fragmentation. Since the 1990s, many intellectuals, politicians and ordinary people have expressed disquiet about what they call *communautarisme* (communitarianism). This describes the dangerous fragmentation of the body politic when faced with multiple and overlapping expressions of religious, ethnic or racial politics. Over time, it has become a catch-all term for French fears about social and political disintegration, as well as a vehicle for all manner of negative stereotypes about British multiculturalism and American 'ghettos'. Its ubiquity is reflected in the fact that, in the last decade, it has been used by political parties of all stripes. Whether in discussions about the European Charter for Regional and Minority Languages or the wearing of headscarves in pre-schools, one of the first words to appear in editorials and television debates is invariably *communautarisme*.

As many scholars have shown, twenty-first-century France is full of different intermediary bodies, from political parties and trade unions to ethnic and faith-based organizations. Their existence is a natural consequence of a highly complex and stratified society, and there is ample evidence that political actors have had to mobilize these groups to win elections and secure power. But these realities coexist with a republican idea of national unity that rejects overt political expressions of difference. The result is that French people, whether in positions of authority or not, are continually navigating between an abstract republican idea of homogeneity and the need to recognize difference in their everyday lives. This tension remains one of the most intractable paradoxes in contemporary France.

The question of national unity has been further exacerbated in recent years by important changes in the way France is governed. At a domestic level, this began in the early 1980s under the socialist government, when significant powers were devolved to new territorial entities called *régions* that were designed to replace the 100 or so *départements* that were created during and after the French Revolution. This process has had a major impact on the way state resources are distributed, with local authorities now far more able to choose how they allocate their budgets. Decentralization has extended beyond metropolitan France as well. The best example of this is New Caledonia, which has held several referendums on whether to remain a part of France or become independent. The most recent, in 2018, led to a 56% vote against independence, but already there have been changes in the relationship between the metropole and its largest Pacific territory. Finally, the gradual integration of French political, economic and legal structures with those of the European Union has – as we will see in the final chapter – transformed the way the country works, from the currency to the nation's borders.

These overlapping forms of devolution – downwards to regions and localities, outwards to

the European Union and the overseas territories –
have inevitably contributed to a sense of dislocation
amongst ordinary French people. One expression of
this has been growing support for the extreme right,
which emphasizes a closed vision of Frenchness.
But another response has been the resurgence of a
republican language of national unity and citizenship.
Thus, the increasingly shrill demands on the part of
many French people that migrants and citizens alike
conform to 'republican values' have not always been
motivated by racism or intolerance. They reflect,
on the contrary, an attempt to preserve the essential
components of what the French call *le vivre-ensemble*
(literally 'living together' or social cohesion). For at
least half a century, this *vivre-ensemble* has depended
upon a shared commitment to republican ideas of citizenship. Likewise, the insistent calls for new kinds of
democratic representation and even a 'Sixth Republic'
are not simply wishful thinking. They reflect a lasting
belief in the power of republican values to shape the
institutions of government. It is this belief that keeps
the flame of republicanism alive and guarantees its
status as one of the foundational languages of French
political culture.

### The Republic's Broken Promises: Race and Gender

Historically, one of the most important features of
French republicanism has been its universalist quality.
Because republican values are anchored in abstract

principles such as equality, liberty, popular sovereignty and freedom of expression, they hold out the promise that they are accessible to all, regardless of origin, colour or creed. This universal reflex explains why the revolutionaries of the late eighteenth century wanted to open the First Republic to enlightened citizens from across the world and, still today, enthusiastic supporters of a republican idea like *laïcité* believe it can (and should) be copied everywhere. As with every universal ideology, however, there is a gap between lofty rhetoric and the messy realities of everyday life. In the case of French republicanism, this has frequently led to claims of hypocrisy. These criticisms have existed since the French Revolution, but they became increasingly audible as republicanism was elevated into a governing ideology in the late nineteenth century. It was one thing to criticize individual supporters of republicanism for their failings; it was quite another when a republican state failed to live up to its own values.

The contradictions of French republicanism have changed in the twenty-first century, but the basic tension between rhetoric and reality remains. Why is it, for instance, that a young black man from a depressed neighbourhood in Lyon should find it so much harder to exercise his right to equality than his middle-aged white counterpart? Why should a young Arab woman wearing a headscarf find that everyone talks to her about *laïcité* when hardly anyone mentions it to the nun who is sitting opposite her in the

Paris metro? And why is it that thousands of hetero-sexual couples adopt children every year but fewer than 10 homosexual couples have done so since adoption by homosexual couples was legalized in 2013? In each case, it is not that France is unusual. On the contrary, discrimination against young black men, women wearing the headscarf and same-sex couples is widespread in Europe. What makes the French case unusual is that these groups often believe that they faithfully embody republican values, only to find themselves chastised by other French people – or the state – for not upholding them adequately. As a result, the battle between marginalized groups and the French state becomes a battle over the meaning of republicanism.

There are many possible ways to explore this prob-lem in modern French history, but there are two par-ticularly striking examples: race and gender. Telling the story of republicanism through these lenses reveals the limits of republican universalism and the flaws, blindspots and inequalities at the heart of republican values.

The history of French republicanism has, from the very start, been entangled with the history of race. Even before the proclamation of the First Republic in 1792, colonized peoples across the French empire recognized the explosive potential of repub-lican values like liberty and equality. The Haitian Revolution illustrated how these values could be used not simply to empower black slaves, but also as a powerful mobilizing force against the imposition of French rule. Haitians realized that, in their purest and most radical form, republican values were incompatible with slavery, indenture and colonialism – and they challenged the French to stand by these universal values. Of course, this is not what happened. Although the Haitians did eventually gain independence, they found themselves under attack by angry French planters – who did not have much interest in republican values anyway and were certainly not about to extend these to black people – and Napoleon's armies. As the Haitians discovered to their cost, French republicanism was only available to a select group of white people who lived in metropolitan France. Everyone else would have to wait before being inducted into the republican community.

This flagrant racial inequality at the heart of French republicanism only became more pronounced in the nineteenth century. There were moments when republicans seemed willing to live up to their principles – for example, the abolition of slavery at the height of the revolution in 1848 – but mostly the promise of republicanism was strictly reserved for the 'evolved races'. This process reached its apogee during the Third Republic when republicanism became a justification for colonialism. At the very moment the French elites were announcing the triumph of republican values in metropolitan France in the 1880s and 1890s, they were using these same values to explain the necessity of the *mission civilisatrice* in the colonies. Colonial officials made grand speeches in which they argued that the imposition of French rule and the establishment of republican institutions like public schools were a fulfilment of the universal ambitions of the Republic. Inevitably, those who experienced colonial expansion saw it differently. For them, a flowery rhetoric of progress and republican enlightenment was little more than a cover for war, expropriation, pillage and persecution.

Yet, despite their overwhelmingly negative experience of French colonialism, many colonized people were able to differentiate between the emancipatory potential of republican rhetoric and its manipulation by colonial elites. Over time, this led to two sharply contrasting visions of the promise of French republicanism. On the one hand, the French continued to argue – at least until the decolonization of Algeria in 1962 – that the universal destiny of the French Republic was compatible with the inequalities of colonialism. On the other, a growing number of colonized people claimed the opposite. They maintained that, after dying for France in two world wars and doing their best to embody the finest values of French republicanism, they had earned the right to self-government and equal treatment.

As we have seen, harsh realities of decolonization finished off dreams of a union of equal peoples across the French empire. Nevertheless, the constitutive racial tension within French republicanism that emerged in the colonial period persisted into the postcolonial period. Of the hundreds of thousands of people who migrated to France from its former colonies, some were already citizens; others were not. But all of them brought their own memories of imperialism, subjugation and emancipation – and they often transmitted these to their children. Today, somewhere between 5 and 8 million people – we do not have exact numbers because the French state prohibits the collection of statistics on ethnic grounds – have some connection with the former French empire. Many of these French people have continued to fight their parents' and grandparents' battles for racial equality and, in particular, they have started to challenge one of the most important tenets of French republicanism: a colour-blind model of citizenship.

Non-white people in France have long known that, whatever their legal status, they are treated like second-class citizens. Abundant research shows that they suffer open racism and violence but also a whole range of less overt forms of discrimination. At an individual level, they get turned away from nightclubs and campsites without reason; they are far more likely to be stopped by the police; and they struggle to break through a variety of negative stereotypes in everyday life. Even when they are physically invisible – as in the case of job applications with no accompanying photos – they find that their names are enough to ring alarm bells. An Omar or a Mustafa is far less likely to get called for a job interview than a Jean-Marc or a Charles. At a structural level, too, it is a major disadvantage to be black or brown. Ethnic minorities in France are more likely than their white counterparts to be unemployed, poor and ill – and they find it difficult to access the necessary public services since their level of educational attainment or mastery of the French language is often lower.

Many countries have tried to deal with similar problems using forms of affirmative action that create quotas for – or give preferential treatment to – those from disadvantaged backgrounds. These are often symbolic and relatively ineffective measures, but they have the benefit of being widely accepted. Not so in France, where any attempt to develop policies that might favour a specific racial, ethnic or religious group is tarred with the brush of *communautarisme*. State officials and public officeholders cannot openly say that a particular social, educational, cultural or economic policy is targeted at the 'Muslim community', 'black people' or 'Moroccans' because it is seen to violate a core tenet of French republicanism. The consequence of this is that such policies are either abandoned or implemented 'silently' without mentioning the group that is being targeted. The former is a problem because it means that nothing changes, but the latter is often worse because it suggests a form of collective denial. It is hard enough to tackle social problems that are visible; it is much harder to deal with those that are shrouded in silence. Perhaps the most striking recent example of republican rhetoric

trying to reshape the reality of racism was the decision by the Assemblée nationale to remove the word
'race' from the first line of the French constitution in
2018. The logic behind this cross-party amendment
was laudable: its supporters argued that the concept
of race had no place in a formal state document. But
people were quick to point out that removing the
word 'race' from the constitution would not magi-
cally make the idea of race disappear from French
society, nor would it do much to help anti-racism
campaigns.

The growing realization that contemporary French
republicanism cannot accommodate racial difference
has led to the creation of a constellation of organizations and protest movements. Since the 2000s,
ethnic minorities have begun to articulate publicly
their ideas about their rights and responsibilities as
citizens, ranging from radical left-wing, anti-racist
movements, through to civil society groups like the
Conseil représentatif des associations noires (CRAN,
Representative Commission of Black Organizations).
In addition, musical genres like hip-hop and raï, as
well as a plethora of books and films produced by
ethnic minorities, have emphasized the specificity of
the non-white experience in France. Many of these
cultural products express deep anger about the historic discrimination suffered by postcolonial immigrants and their children, but they also frequently
highlight the contradictions of French republicanism.
Young people in music videos brandish the ultimate

symbol of citizenship – the *carte d'identité* (identity card) – and demand to know what happened to the country of 'liberty, equality, fraternity'. Rap artists sing about the devastating legacies of slavery. And film-makers draw poignant sketches of France's colonial veterans plunged into poverty because their military pensions were frozen in the 1960s.

There are many ways of reading this flowering of ethnic minority political culture in twenty-first-century France. Some have suggested that it marks the beginning of a full-scale repudiation of French republicanism on the part of alienated ethnic minorities. The series of Islamist attacks that rocked France in 2015 and 2016, many of which were conducted by homegrown terrorists, seemed to confirm this view. Here were young ethnic minorities visibly and violently rejecting the symbols, values and ideals of the French Republic in the name of an alternative universal ideology, that of radical Islam. But a long-term perspective suggests that today's ethnic minorities are not so much rejecting republicanism as demanding that it fulfil its promise. They know that the republicanism that prevents them from expressing their racial or ethnic identity in public is the flipside of the one that promises equality and freedom to all. By telling their stories of endurance and resistance, they want to change the parameters of contemporary French republicanism so that it can accommodate their unique experiences. The Republic may have betrayed them, but it holds within it the kernel of something different, and it is this hope that gives their struggles such intensity.

The battle for women's rights and gender equality in France represents another unfulfilled promise of French republicanism, the origins of which lie in the French Revolution. It was in various pieces of legislation implemented between 1791 and 1793 that women gained formal equality with men, including unprecedented rights to equal inheritance and divorce. Women also featured prominently in revolutionary imagery, and many took to the streets to protest alongside men. But these gains were short-lived. In 1804, Napoleon's Civil Code reversed these changes and unambiguously established women's *incapacité juridique* (legal incapacity). After a brief period during which women were told they could be at the vanguard of revolution, they were relegated back to the legal status of children.

Remarkably, this situation persisted almost unchanged until the end of the Second World War. Not only did the Civil Code continue to form the basis of most family law throughout the nineteenth and early twentieth centuries, but no effort was made to integrate women into political life. This was understandable during the reigns of Napoleon and Napoleon III since political and civil rights for men were also curtailed in these periods. But it is harder to explain why the revolutionary government of 1848 and the nominally republican lawmakers of the Third Republic refused to countenance the integration of women into politics, let alone grant them equal legal rights. It is difficult to imagine now that, for the first half of the twentieth century, there were more black *députés* in the Assemblée nationale than there were women. The only exception was during the Popular Front government in 1936, when Léon Blum invited three women to sit as ministers, even though they could neither vote, nor hold elected office.

The explanation for this rigid resistance on the part of republican men to the enfranchisement of women lay partly in the persistence of strongly patriarchal and Catholic values across French society but mostly in a deep distrust of women's political motivations. The vast majority of politicians under the Third Republic believed that women's *incapacité juridique* extended to politics as well. In their eyes, women were politically immature and susceptible to irrational persuasion. They thought women were easily swayed by their local priest or by a charismatic leader like Napoleon, and they feared that giving them the vote would lead to the collapse of the republican state. Unlike in other European countries, where voting restrictions on women were rapidly lifted after 1918, the French elites remained stubbornly wedded to the view that women could not – and should not – be full citizens of the Republic.

France's wartime experience and the desire for a fresh start made it all but impossible to maintain a strict ban on female participation in politics. Women's suffrage was granted immediately in 1945 and, for the first time, women could hold elected office. But the effects of this change were underwhelming. Women were reticent about participating in the political process, both as electors and as politicians. Abstention rates were consistently higher for women until the 1970s and, after an initial (if modest) rush to stand for election, their numbers declined at all levels of political representation through the 1950s and 1960s. Of the many statistics one could cite, one of the most notable is that, from 1950 to 1980, not more than 5% of the *députés* in the Assemblée nationale were women – and their numbers only exceeded 10% for the first time in 1997.

The dramatic under-representation of women in post-war French politics stood in stark contrast to the flourishing of female intellectual and political life in the same period. Philosophers like Simone de Beauvoir and Hélène Cixous, anti-colonial activists like Germaine Tillion and lawyers like Simone Veil stood at the forefront of some of the most important intellectual innovations and legal changes of their time. They provided the analytical tools with which to dismantle patriarchy, deconstruct masculinity and unpick a sexist legal system. They were also instrumental in pushing for reforms to the Civil Code in the late 1960s and 1970s that led to the equalization of divorce law, positive changes to family and inheritance law, and the legalization of abortion. But these individual figures could not by themselves dismantle the assumption that lay at the heart of French republicanism, namely the belief that the Republic should be built on the foundations of the patriarchal, heterosexual family.

It was only at the end of the twentieth century that activists and intellectuals started to tackle this problem directly. One particularly symbolic piece of legislation that passed in 2000 was the so-called *parité* (parity) law, which stipulated that political parties should present at least 50% of women candidates on their electoral lists. The law applies strictly to every type of election, except for legislative elections, where parties are given a fine if they do not comply. Not surprisingly, the law was staunchly opposed by many people on republican grounds. As in the case of affirmative action policies, critics argued that it was tantamount to introducing a quota for women and therefore contrary to the republican principle of legal equality. Ultimately, the law was only able to pass because its supporters successfully reframed it as a vindication of French republican values. They maintained that, since the difference between men and women was a constitutive division within the French Republic, the law would merely reflect reality, rather than seek to change it by favouring one group at the expense of another. It was a bold and imaginative claim – and one that showed how French republicanism could be reshaped from the inside.

Another example of a public collision between republican values and gender politics has come through a series of debates over homosexual rights.

These three areas have been addressed in different ways through the 1999 law that created the *pacte civil de solidarité* (PACS, civil union), the 2013 law that legalized gay marriage (*mariage pour tous*) and the 2019 law that opened assisted reproductive technologies to single women and same-sex couples. On all three occasions, the legislation was accompanied by bitter political polemic. Many of those who opposed the changes deployed traditional right-wing or religious arguments about the sanctity of marriage as a union between a man and a woman, but these were supplemented by intellectuals, politicians and activists who argued they would contravene republican values. The argument here again was that policies designed for homosexuals would give special rights to a specific community. Moreover, they suggested that the heterosexual family formed the bedrock of French society and, by extension, the social foundation of French republicanism.

The response to these criticisms has been robust – and largely successful. Advocates of the PACS in the late 1990s worked hard to show that it was consistent with republican values by extending the principle of civil union to any two people – heterosexual, homosexual or just partners – wishing to enter a contract with each other. Likewise, legislation related to reproductive rights has been championed not only by the left, but also by Macron's centrist liberal coalition, a clear sign that it no longer offends republican sensibilities in the way that it once did. At a broader level, the emergence of homosexual activist organizations in the 1980s and 1990s did much to expose the heteronormative basis of French republicanism, a process that has had long-term implications for perceptions of women, gender and the family. These days, it is rare for resistance to reform of the family code or gay rights to be articulated on republican grounds.

Nevertheless, there is a long way to go. Political parties still prefer to pay fines rather than abide by the rules on *parité*, and women – especially Muslim women – remain disproportionately affected by the normative injunctions that underpin republican values. Given the glacial pace of change, it is hardly surprising that some women are demanding more vigorous action of the kind that led to the French version of the #MeToo movement, colourfully known as #BalanceTonPorc ("squeal on your pig"). Like radical affirmations of racial difference, these more aggressive forms of gender politics indicate the beginning of a rejection of the more gradualist egalitarian aspirations of republicanism. If the French state and the French elites continue to drag their feet in relation to gender equality, the time may come when women and homosexuals in France abandon their commitment to republican ideals in their ongoing struggle to achieve equality. History suggests, though, that they are far more likely to achieve their aims by rewriting the past and present of French republicanism than by discarding it altogether.

# 6

# Local Citizens in a Global State

On Saturday, 17 November 2018, hundreds of thousands of people donned standard-issue high-visibility yellow vests and occupied roundabouts, sliproads and town squares across France. Their organization was almost entirely spontaneous. Instead of being led by a trade union or a political movement, they mobilized on social media. Nor did they appear to have a clear ideological platform. They seemed to be talking about a whole variety of social issues, from high fuel prices to overstretched public services. Their demands were driven by an emotion – anger – rather than a policy platform. The message was that the *ras-le-bol* (exasperation) of ordinary French people had become untenable. Many expected that the protests would peter out after a month or two, but they were still going a year later. Their size had reduced significantly, and they no longer represented a real political threat, but their lingering presence was a reminder of the depth of the discontent. In their scope and longevity, the *gilets jaunes* became the largest wave of protest since 1968 and one of the few that could claim a genuine nationwide following, from the Champs-Élysées in Paris to the small island of Réunion in the Indian Ocean.

There are many possible interpretations of the *gilets*

*jaunes*. We saw earlier how they embody a tradition of French resistance to arbitrary power and economic injustice. This fits with a widespread sense that they represent a novel form of anti-capitalist movement. Other, more critical commentators have suggested that they mark the start of a mass reaction against unpopular environmental policies. For the historian of modern France, however, the most persuasive interpretation is the one that places them within a longer history of conflictual state–citizen relations. This is because the *gilets jaunes* were, right from the start, focused incessantly on the state. They blamed the state for a multitude of sins, while simultaneously seeking redress from the very same state against which they were so vocally protesting. They demanded lower taxes, less bureaucracy and less state intervention, but also more public spending, more public services and greater subsidies. Even the symbol of the movement was a way of indicting the state. Immediately visible and highly photogenic, the yellow vest must by law be carried inside every vehicle in France. Police routinely stop motorists – often on roundabouts – and dish out fines to those who do not have one. For motorists, the yellow vest represents both state authority and the imposition of unwanted external norms. While few French people question the eminently rational safety logic that underpins the wearing of the yellow vest, many of them resent that it has been foisted on them by an interfering state. In their manipulation of this banal symbol during the *gilets jaunes* protests, they perpetuated a now familiar pattern in French politics, in which citizens angrily reject their own state's attempts to impose policies and ideas that are supposed to be in their best interests.

## Centre and Periphery: Local Challenges to the French State

To outside observers, the French obsession with the state often seems to verge on the pathological. Yet the dynamic and fraught relationship between individual citizens and the state has been an essential part of the French social contract, at least since the late eighteenth century. The enormous expansion of the welfare system after the Second World War reinforced this tendency by tying the fate of huge numbers of French people to a range of state systems, subsidies and policies. The result was that, by the 1970s, the French did more than simply support or oppose the actions of their state; they identified with it. This process has continued into the twenty-first century, but, as the French state has entered a protracted crisis since the 1980s, so too have the French people.

One of the most important reasons for this crisis is the ongoing tension between citizens' local priorities and their state's global ambitions. For a long time, France was held up as the archetypal example of a country with a strong state and fragile citizens' organizations. The relative weakness of trade unions, political parties, civil society associations and the non-governmental sector – especially compared to countries like Germany or the United States – made France seem like a statist exception. The early years of the Fifth Republic appeared to confirm this model, with its strong executive, a sophisticated technocratic state and a long-standing republican hostility to intermediary bodies. Neither mass protests like those led by the anti-tax politician Pierre Poujade in the 1950s or the student and labour unrest of 1968 could dislodge the state from its pre-eminent position at the apex of the French polity. Still today, visitors are surprised by the degree of top-down coordination in sectors such as education and transport. There is a reason why the French so often feel that the state penetrates their daily lives.

But the image of a society strangled by an omnipresent state is only a partial one. There has always been a good deal more local diversity than the statist myth has allowed. For a start, entrenched regional identities have repeatedly challenged the authority of the centralizing state. Delayed industrialization and a powerful agricultural sector ensured that regional attachments were preserved and transmitted throughout the post-war period. Even in the twenty-first century, many French people continue to identify with a region. They return to their local 'roots' during the holidays when they visit their dilapidated family homes, often located in rural areas. Although the economic and political power of urban areas has grown, the development of tourism has given a new lease of life to declining rural areas and some of France's overseas territories. Millions of French people flock to local attractions and consume food or wine that is explicitly marketed as an authentic expression of a particular region or town. Regional cultures also appeal to the enormous number of foreign visitors. While Paris remains the main draw, tourists from the United Kingdom, the Low Countries and Germany – who made up more than 45% of foreign visitors in 2018 – spend significant amounts of time criss-crossing the countryside in search of *la France profonde* (literally, 'deep France'). In some places, struggling rural communities have come to rely almost entirely on seasonal tourism for their survival.

The self-conscious packaging of regional France for outside consumption has not always met with approval. Inhabitants of rural areas and overseas territories have regularly politicized their regional identities in order to draw attention to the realities behind the glossy travel supplements. For example, radical winegrowers' organizations in the south of France initiated direct-action terrorist-style bombings in the 1970s and 1980s. Their targets were big supermarkets and new farming standards imposed by the EEC. For a while, they represented a genuine threat to property in the hinterlands near places like Béziers and Montpellier. Their protests were ultimately a failure, but the fear of coordinated rural unrest left a lasting trace in the form of the French defence of the European Common Agricultural Policy and the frequency with which the state bails out struggling farmers. Other very different examples of politicized regional identities can be found in France's overseas territories. These invariably focus on the much higher rates of poverty and unemployment in these areas compared to metropolitan France. In some places, such as New Caledonia and Corsica, such resentments have fuelled separatist and independence movements. Even where the prospect of a separation from France seems remote, protests in the overseas territories serve to highlight regional specificities and raise questions about the way France is organized.

There was little overt politicization of regional identities amongst the *gilets jaunes*, but the protests were a reminder of the importance of France's geographical periphery. As several commentators noted, there was a striking similarity in aims and methods between the *gilets jaunes* and the protests that paralysed French Guiana a little over a year earlier in March and April 2017, a sign that similar grievances were shared across a wide geographical area and a very diverse population. Moreover, the predominant form of *gilets jaunes* mobilization provided a unique opportunity to recreate interpersonal solidarities that had been damaged by the depopulation or rapid transformation of many rural or semi-rural communities. As much as anything, a weekly gathering on a local roundabout was a way of meeting people and sharing common grievances. The often carnivalesque atmosphere of *gilets jaunes* protests suggests that the movement served an important social function, even when it lacked a clear political strategy. Only time will tell whether the *gilets jaunes* were a harbinger of more cohesive local and regional identities or, on the contrary, a last-ditch attempt to salvage a sense of community in peripheral and neglected areas of France.

The persistence of regional identities is not the only way in which French people have resisted the post-war state. Another crucial, if understudied, phenomenon is the explosion of local organizations – or, as the French call them, *associations*. Under French law, an *association* is any group of more than two people that is organized around a common, non-profitable purpose. This means that there is basically no limit on the form and content of an *association*. They can be anything from trade unions with thousands of members to small gatherings of chess enthusiasts. In order to gain formal recognition, all that is required is for members to make a declaration of the organization's statutes to the relevant public authority. To get an idea of the significance of this phenomenon, one need only look at the statistics. In the early 1960s, around 10,000 to 12,000 new *associations* were founded every year; in the early 1980s, this doubled to approximately 30,000 every year; and, by the mid-2000s, records show that a staggering 70,000 were being created every single year. In 2019, the French state estimated that there were upwards of 1.5 million *associations* across France, the majority of which were focused on sport (24%), art and culture (23%), leisure activities (21%), charity and social services (14%) and the defence of specific causes (12%).

The existence of such a huge constellation of civil society organizations flies in the face of a traditional statist view of France as a country with weak and sub-servient intermediary bodies. Famously, it was Alexis de Tocqueville in the mid-nineteenth century who emphasized the contrast between the vibrant civil society of the United States and the anaemic associa-tive life of France. But, while there are still enormous differences in the way these two countries are organ-ized and run, the contrast between their respective civil societies has narrowed significantly. Statistics provided by the US State Department suggest that there are around 1.5 million non-governmental organizations in the United States. Even allowing for the differences in the way the two states define such entities, it is remarkable that this figure should be the same as France, not least because the population of the United States is more than five times larger than that of France.

The explanation for this impressive growth of civil society in France is both political and socio-logical. Politically, it was closely related to attempts by successive governments from the 1970s onwards to 'democratize' French society. In the wake of the protests of 1968, even the most hardened techno-crats realized that heavy-handed state intervention could not continue; it needed to be tempered by much greater citizen involvement in social life. As we already know, Valéry Giscard d'Estaing, who came to power in 1974, began to loosen the grip of the state and create the conditions for citizens to participate in decision-making processes. The socialist government that came after him in 1981 took this one step further. With many former *soixante-huitards* in its ranks, the PS supercharged existing efforts to emancipate the French from the tutelage of their state by pouring money into art, culture and leisure. New sporting and music venues were inaugurated across the country, and culture festivals began to spring up everywhere. The effects were particularly noticeable in medium-sized provincial towns and cities, which suddenly found themselves playing host to prestigious early music or ballet festivals.

Over time, this proactive cultural policy began to have positive effects on citizens' participation in civic life. What at first had taken the form of massive state subsidies to stimulate the cultural economy gradually reconciled the French to the value of civil society. Experience of managing state-funded initiatives gave ordinary people the confidence to set up their own *associations*, and they began to do so in large numbers. This process was facilitated by imaginative experiments in local government, many of which were led by left-wing politicians. As early as the 1960s, the socialist mayor of Grenoble, Hubert Dubedout, inaugurated the *Groupes d'action municipale* (municipal action groups). These were autonomous, non-partisan groups of citizens who got together to elaborate policies at a local level. Similarly, the maverick socialist mayor of Montpellier, Georges Frêche, created a system of *maisons pour tous* (literally, 'houses for all') in each of the city's neighbourhoods. They brought together in one building many of the key services of local government, as well as youth centres, cultural venues and dedicated office space for *associations*. This sort of initiative cemented the link between the state and civil society and ensured the latter would no longer automatically be subservient to the former.

The development of civil society in the 1970s and 1980s was also a response to sociological changes. The most important of these was the emergence of young people as a distinct group within French society. By the 1960s, the post-war baby boom, the sharp increase in disposable income and the expansion of higher education made 'youth' a prime target market for advertisers and political organizations alike. The French state, too, began to take an interest in youth, especially after the protests of 1968. A range of new policies were rolled out in the 1970s and 1980s, many of which involved the creation of youth centres and organizations. To support this infrastructure, local municipalities created thousands of new jobs for *animateurs* (youth workers). Funding for youth policies reached its apogee under the socialist governments of the 1980s, for whom the enfranchisement of young people was part of a wider project to fashion better and more engaged citizens. As in the case of cultural policy, the legacy of these investments outlived the governments that implemented them. *Animateurs* who had been trained and paid for by the state retained their skills after the money ran out, and they used their expertise to set up *associations* to support young people. Today, local youth-orientated organizations, many of which are run by current or former *animateurs*, have become an essential part of the social fabric in some of the country's poorest urban areas. They are one of the few bright spots in a world of high unemployment, inadequate housing and over-stretched public services.

There is, of course, a less charitable explanation for the development of French civil society in the final decades of the twentieth century. Critics – amongst them the *gilets jaunes* – argue that the only reason so many citizens have taken it upon themselves to set up local organizations is because the state has ceased to perform its primary function as a mechanism for social integration. Under pressure from a neo-liberal critique of the state and a sustained politics of austerity, the creation of *associations* provides welcome relief for local and national authorities who no longer have enough resources to spend. There is some truth to this view. The French state has struggled to keep up with public spending, and it has been mired in a permanent deficit crisis since 1975. In recent years, public debt has reached almost 100% of the gross national product, a clear sign that the state is spending beyond its means. Governments of both the right and left have accepted the need for less public spending, even if they have found it extremely difficult to cut services, pension provisions or infrastructure investment. In such a context, an emphasis on civil society has been a useful way to shift the responsibility for public services on to individuals. Yet this legitimate criticism fails to recognize that, in France, the growth of civil society has not always happened outside – or against – the state. On the contrary, it began as a top-down attempt to give more power to citizens in response to widespread discontent about the post-war technocratic state. Within a decade or two, the state lost control of this process as citizens used their experiences to create their own organizations. In so doing, they transformed the relationship between state and citizen in France. For the first time in modern French history, large numbers of citizens have begun to organize their social, political and cultural activities independent of a major institution, be it the Catholic Church or the state.

This shift has important consequences for the way we analyse French society. The Tocquevillian image of a population labouring under an omnipotent state was never as accurate as it was made out to be, but it is positively misleading today. Yes, the French still have a complex and conflictual relationship with the state. Their propensity to protest at a moment's notice is not simply a symptom of an irrational French 'impatience' or 'anger'; it is a historic response to a state apparatus that is notoriously undemocratic and unrepresentative. But an incessant focus on the state obscures other, equally important, realities. Outsiders tend to think of the French through clichéd character sketches like the striking train driver, the disgruntled schoolteacher or the student on the barricades. These ideal incarnations of Frenchness are all dependent on the state and very likely to be unionized. But there are four times as many French people today who belong to *associations* rather than to trade unions, and even the most archetypal state employees are involved in *associations* themselves. It no longer makes sense to cast the French as uniquely dependent on their state; in their enthusiasm for civil society, they have become much more like their German and American cousins.

The *gilets jaunes* perfectly captured the contemporary tensions between civil society and the state in France. Their rhetoric followed a time-worn pattern. It revolved around the state – its failings, its corruption, its responsibilities. But their organization showed a deep desire to extend local solidarities of the kind that underpinned the growth of civil society in the 1970s and 1980s. Their weekly Saturday lunches mimicked the *fêtes* and gatherings that are a major part of the social calendar in small communities. And their social composition – including far more women than on most protests in France – reflected the changes that have taken place in French society as traditional class and regional differences have fallen away. Scholars and commentators will no doubt continue to argue over how to interpret the *gilets jaunes* – in particular, whether they represented a movement of the left or the right. But one thing is for certain:

they demonstrated that the local citizen is more than ever a powerful force in French politics.

## France's Global Ambitions: Myth or Reality?

One of the biggest challenges facing European states today is how to balance the needs of their citizens with their global ambitions. This problem is especially acute in the case of France. For several centuries, the French considered themselves to be one of the pre-eminent military, political and cultural forces in Europe, if not the world. Even when faced with defeat on the battlefield, they took pride in the prestige of French culture and the French language. From Washington to Saigon, Frenchness was a way of signalling high style and sharp intellect. But this self-perception suffered a severe blow in the middle decades of the twentieth century, with a series of military defeats from 1940 onwards, and the collapse of the French empire in the late 1950s and early 1960s. It was reinforced by a bipolar Cold War system, in which the United States and the Soviet Union were the undisputed superpowers, and a series of embarrassing foreign policy setbacks, starting with the Suez Crisis in 1956. To make matters worse, the international prestige of French culture began to decline. Although Paris was Europe's intellectual capital from the end of the Second World War to the late 1960s, it was soon under threat from cities like London and New York, especially as English began to replace French as the lingua franca of the world's intellectual elites. The same was true of other quintessentially French cultural products. From haute couture to wine, France began to face unprecedented competition from producers elsewhere.

During de Gaulle's presidency in the 1960s, it was possible to ignore some of these realities. A self-conscious policy of *grandeur* made it appear as if the country could still fulfil its destiny as a great power. But the 1970s brought a further diminishing of status as economic stagnation set in and the centres of geopolitical gravity shifted towards regions like the Middle East and East Asia. This confirmed what every observer knew, namely that France was little more than a medium-sized nuclear power, albeit one with memories of a glorious past. But, if many policymakers realized the importance of adapting to a more modest place in the world, the same was not necessarily true of the French people as a whole. The way they have come to terms – or not – with France's increasingly subservient position in the global hierarchy has had important political ramifications. It has affected the state's ability to respond to their demands, and it has made them acutely aware of their marginal place in a world of globalized exchange and mobility. Two issues, in particular, have forced the French to confront the growing tension between the local and the global: France's neo-colonial entanglements and the onward march of European integration.

We saw earlier how the shadow of France's colonial

past gave rise to acrimonious postcolonial 'memory wars' over the history of colonialism. But it also had more concrete manifestations in the form of neo-colonial intervention. Much of this involved manpower, hard cash, political networks or straight-forward economic exploitation. For instance, the French continued to send thousands of people to their former colonies after independence, especially in Africa. Most of them were young men doing an alternative to obligatory military service known as the *service de la coopération*, which was introduced in 1965. This involved working abroad for 16 months, usually for an agency of the French state or an equivalent in the host country. The majority of *coopérants*, as they were known, went as engineers, technical advisers, doctors and teachers. There were over 10,500 of them in the mid-1960s; in 1990, there were still 4,000. Military service was abolished in 1997, but the *service de la coopération* represented a major transfer of technical knowledge and personnel to France's former colonies. This was supplemented by large amounts of money. France served as the principal aid donor for all of Francophone Africa, dispensing millions of francs over several decades. The persistence of a single currency zone – the Communauté financière africaine (CFA) – reinforced this economic relationship. The CFA had been set up in 1945 as a way of stabilizing the currency markets in France's African colonies after the Second World War, but several independent states in West Africa found they could not (or would not) leave it after decolonization. The existence of a currency tied to the franc – and, more recently, to the euro – has maintained a system of two-way economic dependency between France and its former colonies, one which is heavily weighted in favour of France.

Inevitably, free labour, development aid and financial support came with strings attached. Francophone African countries had to give French companies priority access to raw materials such as the recently discovered oil reserves in the Algerian Sahara or uranium supplies in Gabon. They were also expected to maintain compliant regimes. This led the French to support tacitly or openly a raft of dictatorial politicians using a shadowy network of mercenaries and diplomatic backchannels. These actions were sanctioned at the very highest level: the mercurial Jacques Foccart – a special minister in charge of relations with Africa for long periods between the 1960s and the 1990s – was literally based inside the Elysée Palace. At his behest, the French sent logistical assistance to friendly leaders like Omar Bongo in Gabon and Hissène Habré in Chad and made sure that political opponents were crushed or marginalized. The aim was always to allow the French to preserve their regional influence, but it was an arrangement that worked for many African leaders as well. With the French as their alibis and protectors, they could easily fend off accusations of corruption or repression.

This symbiotic relationship between France and its former African colonies began to come apart in the

1990s. The end of the Cold War removed one of the most important ideological covers for French interference: the threat of communism. It also strengthened a global discourse of human rights and democracy. One consequence of this was a wave of protest across sub-Saharan Africa, which led to the collapse of several long-standing dictators and one-party regimes. African states gained more economic freedom as they could seek investments without being constrained by their association with one or other of the Cold War superpowers. In particular, the penetration of China into the African economy had a profound impact on France's ability to exercise economic leverage in its sphere of influence. By the late 1990s, France's relationship with its former colonies was under severe scrutiny. At home, the state faced accusations that its neo-colonial policies towards Africa – dubbed 'la Françafrique' – had turned a blind eye to massive human rights abuses committed by French-supported dictators. And in Africa, the French connection disintegrated as leaders looked elsewhere for economic and political allies.

The French response to this decline in influence has taken several forms. One is straightforward disengagement. Successive presidents, starting with Nicolas Sarkozy in 2007, have announced the 'end' of the Françafrique system. Aid and assistance have been withdrawn; the top executives of French companies operating in Africa have been dragged to court and found guilty of corruption, most famously in the case of the oil giant Elf in 1994; and the network of special advisers that underpinned the country's Africa policy has been dismantled. In recent years, the French state has even contemplated forms of restitution for the violence of colonialism. On his various visits to Africa, Macron has come close to apologizing for imperial conquest and is seriously exploring the possibility of returning African artefacts held in French museums. He has also announced the end of the CFA. As late as the 1990s, such policies would have been unthinkable. Every president of the Fifth Republic until 2007 was somehow connected to the history of French colonialism. An apology or compensation would have been tantamount to a personal admission of guilt. These taboos are much weaker today; most people in France, from the president downwards, recognize that colonialism belongs firmly to the past.

The difficulty is that half a century of postcolonial entanglements cannot be dissolved unilaterally. The relationship between France and its former colonies was never equal, but it served the interests of both sides. From the 1990s onwards, the leaders of Francophone African countries no longer looked to France as their main Western donor, but they still called upon a residual French sense of 'responsibility' when it suited them. Thus, the majority of French military operations since 2000 have continued to be in Francophone Africa. French forces were posted for more than a decade in Chad in the 1980s and 1990s, and in Côte d'Ivoire and the Central African

Republic in the 2000s. In 2013, the Malian government requested French support in their battle against a Tuareg insurgency in the north of the country, which was exploited by Islamic jihadi organizations. This intervention morphed into Operation Barkhane, an ongoing multilateral anti-terrorist campaign in the southern Sahara, led by the French.

While these interventions have helped France to retain a foothold in its sphere of influence, they have been costly and unpopular with the French electorate. Each time the state has agreed to send its armed forces to a distant country it has faced one of two accusations: either that such behaviour is merely airbrushed neo-colonial posturing, or that African leaders are playing on the guilt of their former colonial masters. But the truth of the matter is less sinister. As in other areas, France's policies towards its former colonies are riven by contradictions. On the one hand, there is a rhetorical commitment to *grandeur*, a global mission and a post-imperial 'Francophonie'. On the other, the French state does not have the resources or political will to maintain its vast presence indefinitely. It continues to fund an extraordinary network of French institutes, French schools and French consular services in almost every country in the world, but this cultural diplomacy cannot hide the fact that France is not the great power it once was.

The same tensions run through French policies and attitudes towards European integration. From its inception, the French saw the European project as a means of restoring their pre-eminent place in European politics after the Second World War and of controlling Germany's political ambitions. This vision was tenable so long as European integration was limited to a small number of countries, all of which were either politically subservient to France (Benelux and Italy) or geopolitically weakened (West Germany). As soon as the European project began to take in other countries – most importantly, the United Kingdom in 1973, Greece in 1981 and Spain and Portugal in 1986 – the French began to lose their leading role. The reunification of Germany in 1991 and the expansion of the European Union to the former communist countries of Eastern Europe in the 1990s and 2000s shattered what was left of French hegemony. Today, France remains one of the leading players on the European scene. But it cannot hold every other European country to ransom, as it did during the Empty Chair Crisis in 1965 when de Gaulle's refusal to endorse proposed reforms to the governance of the EEC brought European government business to a standstill.

The French have adapted to these changing realities of European integration by shifting from a policy of hard power to one of political influence. This process began in the early 1970s with the accession of the United Kingdom to the EEC. De Gaulle had long suspected that British membership would be a problem for France, and he vetoed its application to join in both 1963 and 1967. De Gaulle's successors, Georges

Pompidou and Valéry Giscard d'Estaing, were less categorical, and they helped smooth the way for Britain to join the EEC after de Gaulle's death. Mired in a deep economic crisis when it joined, the United Kingdom did not initially seem to be much of a threat. But, under the stewardship of Margaret Thatcher from 1979 onwards, the British economy recovered, and the British state embraced neo-liberal economics at almost exactly the same time as the French elected the most left-wing government in Western Europe in 1981.

A clash between such divergent political ideologies was almost inevitable, and many of the bitterest disputes between France and Britain in recent decades have taken place in the corridors of European power in Brussels and Strasbourg. For example, Mitterrand's decision to focus on Europe after his government's economic about-turn in 1983 – and especially the decade-long tenure of French socialist Jacques Delors as president of the European Commission from 1985 to 1995 – provided ample opportunity for conflict. The British and French sparred over budget rebates, monetary policy and the Common Agricultural Policy. One of Thatcher's most famous speeches was held at the College of Europe in Bruges in September 1988. In a celebrated passage, she said, 'We have not successfully rolled back the frontiers of the state in Britain, only to see them re-imposed at a European level with a European super-state exercising a new dominance from Brussels.' This was a direct response to Delors's espousal of a 'social Europe' that would extend some of the most cherished social policies of French socialism to the entire European Community. Both Mitterrand and Delors recognized that they could not order their European partners to comply with their wishes as de Gaulle did in the 1960s, but they nevertheless sought to impose French 'values'. Unfortunately, they faced a formidable opponent in Thatcher and the British.

Relations with Germany were never as conflictual as with the British, but reunification was still a major headache for the French. It made Germany into Europe's largest state and changed the Cold War geopolitical balance that had given France so much leverage. As the German economy recovered from the costs of reunification, it also began to set the economic agenda for Europe as a whole. High productivity, low unemployment and a small public debt became the model for the rest of Europe. This was a problem for France, which had high levels of unemployment and spiralling debt. In recent years, France has repeatedly violated the economic restrictions placed on Eurozone economies by the European Central Bank. At the height of the European sovereign debt crisis in 2012, many economists believed France would follow Greece to the brink of default. Given that the premise of the European project was to constrain Germany after the Second World War, there was a bitter irony for the French in being given an economic lesson by their neighbours.

The shifting dynamics within the European Union

since the 1990s have affected French power in other ways too. The accession of Eastern European countries in the 2000s challenged the legitimacy of such cherished French initiatives as the Common Agricultural Policy, while the exigencies of monetary union and political integration have gradually drawn power away from Paris. The latter has had important consequences for the shape of French law and politics, and it has also led to a growing hostility towards the European project. The French only narrowly voted for the Maastricht Treaty in a referendum in 1992 (50.8% in favour) and, in 2005, they shocked the continent by voting down a proposal for a European Constitution (54.7% against). The 'no' campaign succeeded in mobilizing the French electorate's fears about neo-liberalism, globalization, 'Anglo-Saxon' capitalism and a loss of French sovereignty. Then and now, few French people support a unilateral exit from the European Union – although the extreme right regularly toys with the idea of 'Frexit' – but criticisms of Europe have become much more audible in the past decade, largely as a result of anxiety about France's reduced status.

Not everyone in France is worried about Europe, though. In the same way that a significant proportion of the electorate believe that France should stop meddling in the affairs of its former colonies, many have enthusiastically embraced the political and cultural dimensions of European integration. Since the 1950s, the French have actively participated in educational and youth exchange schemes across Europe. Today, France is the number one beneficiary of EU Erasmus student funding – more than 56,000 students went on an Erasmus exchange in 2018 – and the overwhelming majority of the governing elite have some experience in another European country or one of the branches of EU administration. Amongst other things, this internationalization has manifested itself in a huge improvement in the standard of English in recent decades, as young people have looked for ways to participate in global conversations about politics, business and culture. Within EU institutions, the French have jealously defended the use of French as an official language, but at international gatherings they readily communicate in other languages.

The French can also fairly claim that the contemporary architecture of the EU has been strongly influenced by their priorities and interests. It was during Delors's presidency that several key structures were put in place such as economic and monetary union, improved workers' rights and a system of consumer rights. These were not exclusively French proposals, but they were clearly related to Delors's background as a French socialist. Moreover, the continued existence of the increasingly unpopular Common Agricultural Policy – which benefits French farmers more than any others in Europe – is almost entirely due to a concerted effort on the part of French diplomats and administrators to guarantee its future. Since the financial crisis of 2008, few people doubt that Germany has become the dominant European power, but the French are responsible for many of Europe's institutional structures and policies. There is even the possibility that the importance of France in Europe will grow again in the coming years. With Britain outside the EU, there is likely to be a rebalancing of power around a renewed Franco-German axis. France may not be the pre-eminent power it once was, but the EU – and, above all, the Eurozone – is unthinkable without its prestige, military power and political clout. European institutions are full of French officials, the European courts and central banks draw extensively on French expertise and every major reform needs French assent in some form or another. As the EU emerges from a uniquely difficult period in its history, a French 'vision' of Europe may once again prove to be influential in shaping its future.

Such a turnaround would not, however, resolve the fundamental tension between the French state's pursuit of global power and French citizens' yearning for more local and tangible forms of government. For a long time, the French state has tried to persuade people that there is no contradiction between the two. It has asked the French to believe that the president of a local sporting *association* could also spend a year as an Erasmus student in Estonia, or that a local councillor from a small town in Mayotte could also be a Member of the European Parliament. But these myths could only survive for so long. Fewer and fewer French people today trust the state's global ambitions.

Instead, they think that it should focus its efforts closer to home. They would rather see, for example, investment in small rural surgeries than astronomical spending on spectacular rail tunnels under the Alps. The problem is that this sort of policy would raise complicated issues about equity and distribution. Should the French state prioritize the old lady in a small village so that she does not have to drive an extra 20 minutes to pick up her medicines? Or should it support the young French professional who relies on high-speed trains to visit his Italian partner in Milan? There is no easy answer to this conundrum, but the future of France rests on its ability to draw up a new social contract that can reverse the growing divergence between an avowedly global state and its proudly local citizens.

# Conclusion:
# An Uncertain Future

As I write, France finds itself mired in what is likely to become its biggest crisis since the end of the Second World War. The COVID-19 pandemic has taken away lives, destroyed the economy and shattered many of the certainties that people took for granted. In the space of a few months, the major social conflicts and political upheavals of recent years – from the tumultuous presidential election of 2017 to the *gilets jaunes* protests – have receded into the distance. They have been replaced by a new kind of anxiety, focused on an invisible virus and its uncontrollable spread. The French now find themselves locked in a global struggle to contain something that was, until recently, little more than the subject of dystopian science-fiction films and pessimistic government reports that were largely ignored by the general public.

The speed with which COVID-19 has descended on France, Europe and the world is a salutary lesson for historians and social scientists about predictions. We simply do not know what is coming next – and, in the current climate, it would be extremely unwise to guess where a country like France will be in 2, 5 or 20 years' time. But a profound and justifiable sense of uncertainty about the future does not invalidate the arguments in this book. As we have seen time and again, the future of France has been built on – and in conversation with – the past. Many ideas, person-alities and social structures have persisted through catastrophic circumstances, only to come back years – sometimes decades – later. It makes sense, then, to devote this conclusion to four of the most striking patterns, constraints and unresolved questions that emerge out of my narrative of French history since 1940. Whether or not COVID-19 sets in motion irreversible political and economic change, these will necessarily continue to structure public life for the foreseeable future, and they will shape the way the French respond to the unprecedented social and political challenges that lie ahead.

I want first to return to the problem of history and memory. As will be clear by now, France is an intensely historical place. Many European countries remain in constant dialogue with their history, but France is unusual in the depth and diversity of its engagement with the past. Public spaces and public debate are sat-urated with history – its physical manifestations, its bloody victims, its controversies and its ambiguities. French political culture, in particular, is often over-whelmed by references to the past. Politicians seek-ing to defend or attack a specific policy might end up invoking Charlemagne, Napoleon, the revolutionary Terror and the protests of 1968 (though not usually at the same time). In the same vein, French intellectu-als almost always manipulate history in their writings, and even everyday discussions about subjects such as football or pop music can easily veer off into a battle over historical memory.

This incessantly historical mindset has its advantages. First, it ensures that history is a part of daily life and that French people remain aware of its lessons. Second, the memory of past events can have a powerful mobilizing effect. This explains why political figures and movements are so quick to lean on a historical reference point like the Paris Commune or the myth of de Gaulle. Finally, the omnipresence of history ensures that few controversies remain silent for long. There are many things one could say about the way the French have handled the difficult memories of the French Revolution, the Second World War or the Algerian War, but no one can accuse them of not confronting the skeletons in their closet. It may have taken time for each one of these historical moments to become a subject of public attention, but, once they did, there was no way to stop the cascade of opinions and disagreements. The pressure of history was simply too great.

But the bleeding of the past into the present is not without its dangers. The most serious of these is a tendency to ignore uncomfortable contemporary realities. This is clearly visible in the renewed interest in French republicanism in recent decades. While politicians have competed endlessly to embody the eternal 'spirit' of the Republic and intellectuals have quibbled over the correct interpretation of *laïcité*, real social issues like unemployment and racism have gone unresolved. It is sometimes hard to avoid the feeling that it would be easier for many public officials – from teachers to mayors – to do their jobs if they did not continuously have to find ways to conform to France's republican values. The paradox is that it is often these very people who see themselves as the guardians of the republican tradition, with a responsibility not just to the present, but also to the past. They are trapped, like the French people as a whole, in a history of their own making.

The power of history in France is tightly related to the second theme I want to highlight, namely the battle over citizenship. This has become more intense since the 1980s under pressure from waves of postcolonial migration, the emergence of postcolonial identity politics and the atrophy of some of the country's most powerful institutions and ideologies. The question of who a citizen should be and on what terms is now one of the most important debates in contemporary France. Newspapers, blogs and TV chat shows are filled with people arguing over whether Muslims should have to 'do' more in order to be fully French, whether the public funding of mosques and imams violates secular principles, and whether French people can retain their 'identity' within the European Union. The issue is rarely one of legal status. Unlike in many other countries, where there are controversies about who is granted citizenship, the focus in France is usually on people who are already citizens since citizenship is seen as a continuous process, rather than a one-off event.

There are several possible explanations for the prevalence of such debates. An optimistic take is that they reflect an unprecedented extension of the boundaries of citizenship in the twenty-first century. In this reading, traditionally marginalized groups – from same-sex couples to the sons of West African immigrants – have found imaginative ways to reshape what it means to be French. There has been resistance to the integration of these groups, but this has eventually been overcome. In the process, the state has made it possible for same-sex couples to start a family, and the French have learned to dance to *zouglou* music from Côte d'Ivoire. These things would have been hard to imagine even a generation ago, which is proof that open discussions over the terms of citizenship can lead to greater inclusion and a genuine sense of unity in diversity.

The pessimistic view is that most debates over citizenship are about excluding as many people as possible from the national community. There is good evidence to support this position as well. By making citizenship ever more dependent on republican values, the French have limited the definition of the citizen to those who are most able to conform. While well-educated white families living in cities have access to the best of the French welfare and school system, those who live at the geographical or racial periphery struggle to exercise their full rights as citizens. The latter are repeatedly asked to embody republican values but are unable to do so because of their socio-economic circumstances or because they face persistent discrimination. Eventually, they become second-class citizens. This makes them vulnerable to accusations that they are not sufficiently 'integrated', which in turn fuels the rhetoric of politicians like Marine Le Pen, who imply that they are not entirely French.

Whichever interpretation seems more convincing, there can be no discussion of citizenship without a parallel discussion of my third theme: the past and future of the French state. As we saw in the final chapter, the French continue to be deeply attached to the state. They identify strongly with it, and they readily complain about its perceived failures. At the same time, they have played an active role in the expansion of civil society in recent decades. This process was initially welcomed by policymakers, technocrats and politicians. They saw it as a way to reduce the burden on the state, encourage greater participation in civic life and reconfigure relations between the state and citizens. But, in recent years, it has become clear that the disengagement of the state from certain areas has created a strong sense of alienation. This poses a threat to the social and economic fabric of the country, as well as the meaning of citizenship.

The warnings were already there in the *banlieue* unrest in the 1990s and 2000s. Residents of these deprived urban zones were the first to feel the full force of state neglect. This was the precursor to a more general sense of malaise and *ras-le-bol* as the French have begun to worry about their livelihoods, their futures and the disillusionment of their fellow citizens. Such concerns have been reflected in the language of presidential election campaigns. On each occasion, the most promising candidates assert that they will make the French feel 'proud' of themselves again, but no one believes them. Brief moments of enthusiasm for a particular person or policy soon give way to cynicism and tumbling approval ratings. Perhaps the most colourful recent expression of this sense of perpetual gloom was the story of a 73-year-old man who climbed a high-tension electricity pylon in southern France in 2015 and attached a banner demanding the return of de Gaulle. Unfortunately, it was a futile exercise: not only did the General remain firmly in his grave, but the elderly man's ill-advised attempt at historical escapism did not result in even a single power cut.

The French state, too, has lost the self-confidence it once had. From the 1970s onwards, the ideology of modernization that underpinned post-war reconstruction came under sustained attack from across the political spectrum. The advent of neo-liberalism further eroded the principle of state intervention, as did a widespread feeling that individual states were powerless to control global capital flows and financial transactions. These cumulative setbacks meant that, by the 2000s, the French state – like many of its European counterparts – was trapped in a negative spiral. The technocrats, *fonctionnaires* (civil servants) and policymakers who swelled its ranks continued to work hard under difficult circumstances, but they lacked the sense of vocation and mission of their post-war predecessors. Similarly, the infrastructure of the state – from pensions to railways – continued to expand, but without adequate resources or a strong underlying rationale. It is surely not a good thing that most French people today see the state as a necessary evil rather than a generous benefactor.

Its problems notwithstanding, there is no indication that the French state is about to disappear. If anything, the COVID-19 crisis has given it a new lease of life as the creditor, debtor and employer of last resort. But, even in the midst of a pandemic, this renewed commitment to and dependence on the state is unlikely to put an end to my fourth and final theme: the spectre of protest. The diversity of protest in post-war France, especially in comparison to other European countries, has been a consistent thread throughout this book. From the anti-colonial uprisings of the late 1940s to the strikes against Macron's pension reforms at the end of 2019, protest is a constitutive and enduring part of French public life. The most reliable statistics indicate that there have been at least 1,000 protests a year in France since the early 1990s, the equivalent of around three distinct protests every day. Traditionally, the culture of protest has been most readily associated with the French left, but the right has made a nuisance of itself as well. The angry battle cries of embittered French settlers during the Algerian War and the impressive marches by young Catholics during the anti-gay marriage mobilizations in 2013 were no less substantial than similar protests organized by their left-wing counterparts. Whatever the venue, whatever the cause, the French eventually find a way to protest for or against it.

Many commentators and scholars see the French penchant for protest as a prime example of the country's social and political pathologies. They maintain that protest – and the fear of protest – has resulted in a 'stalemate society'. Such an argument reinforces the sense that the main point of protest is not the issue against which people are protesting, but the act of protest itself. This is what the great sociologist Raymond Aron meant when he dismissed 1968 as a 'psychodrama'. As far as he was concerned, the students on the barricades were merely play-acting revolution by simulating the ghosts of protests past. In fact, he argued, conditions in France were exceptionally good, especially compared to many countries in Eastern Europe at the time. Not only was it futile to attempt to overthrow the Gaullist state, it was also dangerous. Why, he asked, would anyone want to tear down a sensible and stable political regime?

In one sense, Aron was right. What happened in Prague in 1968 *was* worse than anything that happened in Paris the same year, and conditions really *were* exceptionally good in France in the late 1960s. But, in another sense, he completely missed the point.

The millions of students and workers who took part in the protests of 1968 were not naïve or foolish. They saw clearly that they lived in a time of plenty and prosperity. What they wanted was to think differently about the way society was organized. By taking on established hierarchies in the university or the factory, they hoped to encourage people to change the way they conducted their daily lives. Most of them were aware that this was a utopian and almost certainly unattainable goal, but they tried it anyway.

There are many parallels between 1968 and 2020. Until the COVID-19 outbreak spiralled out of control, France was – objectively speaking – a prosperous, stable and relatively equal country, with good public health and social security. And yet there was a gnawing sense that something was wrong. French people were worried about things like the decline of the French language, the persistence of unemployment and the threat of globalization. In response, some of them took to the streets, while others cast votes for the extreme right, but almost none of them saw a way out of their predicament. Unlike in 1968, when protesters imagined alternative societies and lifestyles, the overwhelming response in France in recent years has been to defend the status quo. There is nothing intrinsically wrong with this; there is much that is worth saving. But such a defensive reflex automatically casts France as a fragile entity that needs to be protected. This leaves nowhere to go except backwards. It might be time for the French to let go of some of their attachment to the past and focus their energy on imaginative ideas for the future. If the history of modern France is anything to go by, this sort of conversation will be messy and divisive, and it is unlikely to be made any easier by the lingering after-effects of a global pandemic. But there is no other way out of the current impasse. Now, more than ever, the French need to find a way of adhering to one of the most famous slogans of 1968: 'Be realistic, demand the impossible.'

# Further Reading

There is a wonderful array of writing about modern French history. I have selected here only a handful of texts. The idea is to help curious readers who would like to follow up on some of the themes in the book. For reasons of space, I have only included publications available in English, but I cannot stress enough that much of the best work on France is in French. I would urge anyone with an interest in France to develop at least a reading knowledge of French. This is the only way to access the literary and scholarly output of one of the most self-consciously intellectual societies in the world.

My over-arching arguments have been influenced in various ways by Theodore Zeldin, *A History of French Passions* (five vols, 1973–7), Sudhir Hazareesingh, *How the French Think: An Affectionate Portrait of an Intellectual People* (2016), Robert Gildea, *The Past in French History* (1994), and the collection of essays published in English as Edward Berenson, Vincent Duclert and Christophe Prochasson (eds), *The French Republic: History, Values, Debates* (2011). Curious readers will find an extraordinary range of insights in these different books, some of which support my conclusions, others of which contradict them entirely.

The best single-volume English-language history of France during the Second World War is Julian Jackson, *France: The Dark Years, 1940–44* (2001). This can be supplemented by two classic texts on Vichy: Robert Paxton, *Vichy France: Old Guard and New Order, 1940–44* (1972) and Henry Rousso, *The Vichy Syndrome: History and Memory in France since 1944* (1987; English edition, 1994). To get a sense of everyday life in occupied France, I recommend, amongst others, H. R. Kedward, *In Search of the Maquis: Rural Resistance in Southern France 1942–1944* (1993), Hanna Diamond, *Fleeing Hitler: France 1940* (2008) and Shannon Fogg, *The Politics of Everyday Life in Vichy France: Foreigners, Undesirables and Strangers* (2009). The persecution of the Jews is discussed in depth in Michael R. Marrus and Robert Paxton, *Vichy France and the Jews* (1981). On the memories of the Second World War, see Sarah Farmer, *Martyred Village: Commemorating the 1944 Massacre at Oradour-sur-Glane* (2000), Richard Golsan, *The Papon Affair: Memory and Justice on Trial* (2000) and Pieter Lagrou, 'Victims of Genocide and National Memory: Belgium, France and the Netherlands 1945–65', in *Past and Present* (1997).

There has been a remarkable blossoming of research on the French empire in the last two decades. For a clear introduction to the big questions, see Martin Thomas, *Fight or Flight: Britain, France, and Their Roads from Empire* (2013), and, for a single-volume introduction to the Algerian War, Martin Evans, *Algeria:*

*France's Undeclared War* (2007). Todd Shepard, *The Invention of Decolonization: The Algerian War and the Remaking of France* (2006) develops a challenging argument about the contradictions surrounding the decolonization of Algeria. Other parts of the French empire are well dealt with in Tony Chafer, *The End of Empire in French West Africa: France's Successful Decolonization?* (2002), Pierre Brocheux and Daniel Hémery, *Indochina: An Ambiguous Colonization, 1858–1954* (2001; English edition, 2009) and Kristen Childers, *Seeking Imperialism's Embrace: National Identity, Decolonization and Assimilation in the French Caribbean* (2016). Jim House and Neil MacMaster, *Paris 1961: Algerians, State Terror and Memory* (2006), Andrea Smith, *Colonial Memory and Postcolonial Europe: Maltese Settlers in Algeria and France* (2006) and Claire Eldridge, *From Empire to Exile: History and Memory within the Pied-Noir and Harki Communities, 1962–2012* (2016) are excellent case studies of the fractured memory of colonialism in France.

There have been a number of thought-provoking books on the 'Trente Glorieuses'. Good places to start are Herrick Chapman, *France's Long Reconstruction: In Search of the Modern Republic* (2018) and Philip Nord, *France's New Deal: From the Thirties to the Postwar Era* (2012). On the importance of youth, see Richard Ivan Jobs, *Riding the New Wave: Youth and the Rejuvenation of France after the Second World War* (2007). Given his stature, it should come as no surprise that Charles de Gaulle is one of the most written-about figures in

French history. These three texts should, however, give a comprehensive sense of the man and his legacy: Julian Jackson, *A Certain Idea of France: The Life of Charles de Gaulle* (2018), Sudhir Hazareesingh, *In the Shadow of the General: Modern France and the Myth of de Gaulle* (2012) and the relevant chapters in Stanley Hoffmann, *Decline or Renewal? France since the 1930s* (1974).

There is no entirely satisfactory single-volume account of 1968 in English, but there are many very good analyses of different aspects of the protests and their aftermath. These include Michael Seidman, *The Imaginary Revolution: Parisian Students and Workers in 1968* (2004), Daniel A. Gordon, *Immigrants and Intellectuals: May '68 and the Rise of Anti-Racism in France* (2012), Kristin Ross, *May '68 and Its Afterlives* (2002) and Julian Bourg, *From Revolution to Ethics: May 1968 and Contemporary French Thought* (2007). On the post-war French left more generally, see, amongst others, Tony Judt, *Marxism and the French Left: Studies on Labour and Politics in France, 1830–1981* (1986) and Sunil Khilnani, *Arguing Revolution: The Intellectual Left in Postwar France* (1993).

The classic study of the right in France is René Rémond, *The Right Wing in France: From 1815 to de Gaulle* (1954; English edition, 1969). The only recent equivalent in English, although it deals with an earlier period, is Kevin Passmore, *The Right in France: From the Third Republic to Vichy* (2012). For the Gaullist right, Andrew Knapp, *Gaullism since de Gaulle* (1994) is extremely useful. Far and away the best discussion of the post-war extreme right in English is James Shields, *The Extreme Right in France: From Pétain to Le Pen* (2007). For a more obviously political take, see Jim Wolfreys and Peter Fysh, *The Politics of Racism in France* (1998).

There are a variety of ways in which to tackle the interrelated questions of republicanism, national identity and integration in contemporary France. Alec Hargreaves, *Multi-Ethnic France: Immigration, Politics, Culture and Society* (2007) provides a clear introduction. Those interested in politics and ideas can look at Gérard Noiriel, *The French Melting Pot: Immigration, Citizenship and National Identity* (1988; English edition, 1996), Adrian Favell, *Philosophies of Integration: Immigration and the Idea of Citizenship in France and Britain* (1998) and my own book, *A Divided Republic: Nation, State and Citizenship in Contemporary France* (2015). Those keen to know more about the texture of daily life in multicultural France will learn a great deal from Beth Epstein, *Collective Terms: Race, Culture and Community in a State-Planned City in France* (2011) and Julie Kleinman, *Adventure Capital: Migration and the Making of an African Hub in Paris* (2019), both of which offer anthropological reflections on social integration in France. For a more journalistic perspective, I warmly recommend François Maspéro, *Roissy Express: A Journey through the Paris Suburbs* (1990; English edition, 1994), which includes evocative photographs by Anaïk Frantz. The multi-faceted relationship between Jews and Muslims in postcolonial France is treated with sensitivity in Maud Mandel, *Muslims and Jews in France: History of a Conflict* (2014). On Islam and *laïcité*, some of the best work includes John Bowen, *Why the French Don't Like Headscarves: Islam, the State and the Public Space* (2007), Cécile Laborde, *Critical Republicanism: The Hijab Controversy in Political Philosophy* (2008) and Mayanthi Fernando, *The Republic Unsettled: Muslim French and the Contradictions of Secularism* (2014). Two of the most imaginative recent contributions to the ongoing debate about republicanism and gender are Joan Scott, *Parité: Sexual Equality and the Crisis of French Universalism* (2005) and Camille Robcis, *The Law of Kinship: Anthropology, Psychoanalysis, and the Family in France* (2013).

Those interested in France's relations with the outside world have a variety of different approaches from which to choose. Robert Tombs and Isabelle Tombs, *That Sweet Enemy: The French and the British from the Sun King to the Present* (2006) is a magisterial single-volume account of the Franco-British relationship in all its complexity. On Europe, the best one-stop overview is Michael Sutton, *France and the Construction of Europe, 1944–2007* (2007). For contrasting perspectives on Franco-American relations, see Richard Kuisel, *Seducing the French: The Dilemma of Americanization* (1993) and Jean-Philippe Mathy, *Extrême-Occident: French Intellectuals and America* (1994).

Finally, I would encourage anyone interested in contemporary political thought, the history of democracy and theories of the state to look up the writings of Pierre Rosanvallon, Claude Lefort, Marcel Gauchet, Étienne Balibar, Alain Badiou and Michel Crozier, as well as those of more famous thinkers such as Raymond Aron, Pierre Bourdieu and Michel Foucault. Although many of these figures went on to have international careers, they began by writing about their own country and often continued to do so throughout their lives. I have found all of them indispensable to my understanding of contemporary France.

# Index